OPPOSING VIEWPOINTS®

CRIMINAL JUSTICE

Tamara L. Roleff, *Book Editor*

Daniel Leone, *President*
Bonnie Szumski, *Publisher*
Scott Barbour, *Managing Editor*
Helen Cothran, *Senior Editor*

San Diego • Detroit • New York • San Francisco • Cleveland
New Haven, Conn. • Waterville, Maine • London • Munich

For more information, contact
Greenhaven Press
27500 Drake Rd.
Farmington Hills, MI 48331-3535
Or you can visit our Internet site at http://www.gale.com

LIBRARY OF CONGRESS CATALOGING-IN-PUBLICATION DATA

Criminal justice / Tamara L. Roleff, book editor.
p. cm. — (Opposing viewpoints series)
Includes bibliographical references and index.
ISBN 0-7377-1678-9 (pbk. : alk. paper) — ISBN 0-7377-1677-0 (lib. : alk. paper)
1. Criminal justice, Administration of—United States. I. Roleff, Tamara L., 1959– . II. Opposing viewpoints series (Unnumbered)
HV9950.C74324 2003
364—dc21 2002045479

Printed in the United States of America

> "Congress shall make no law. . . abridging the freedom of speech, or of the press."

First Amendment to the U.S. Constitution

The basic foundation of our democracy is the First Amendment guarantee of freedom of expression. The Opposing Viewpoints Series is dedicated to the concept of this basic freedom and the idea that it is more important to practice it than to enshrine it.

Contents

Why Consider Opposing Viewpoints?

"The only way in which a human being can make some approach to knowing the whole of a subject is by hearing what can be said about it by persons of every variety of opinion and studying all modes in which it can be looked at by every character of mind. No wise man ever acquired his wisdom in any mode but this."

John Stuart Mill

In our media-intensive culture it is not difficult to find differing opinions. Thousands of newspapers and magazines and dozens of radio and television talk shows resound with differing points of view. The difficulty lies in deciding which opinion to agree with and which "experts" seem the most credible. The more inundated we become with differing opinions and claims, the more essential it is to hone critical reading and thinking skills to evaluate these ideas. Opposing Viewpoints books address this problem directly by presenting stimulating debates that can be used to enhance and teach these skills. The varied opinions contained in each book examine many different aspects of a single issue. While examining these conveniently edited opposing views, readers can develop critical thinking skills such as the ability to compare and contrast authors' credibility, facts, argumentation styles, use of persuasive techniques, and other stylistic tools. In short, the Opposing Viewpoints Series is an ideal way to attain the higher-level thinking and reading skills so essential in a culture of diverse and contradictory opinions.

In addition to providing a tool for critical thinking, Opposing Viewpoints books challenge readers to question their own strongly held opinions and assumptions. Most people form their opinions on the basis of upbringing, peer pressure, and personal, cultural, or professional bias. By reading carefully balanced opposing views, readers must directly confront new ideas as well as the opinions of those with whom they disagree. This is not to simplistically argue that everyone who reads opposing views will—or should—change his or her opinion. Instead, the series enhances readers' understanding of their own views by encouraging confrontation with opposing ideas. Careful examination of others' views can lead to the readers' understanding of the logical inconsistencies in their own opinions, perspective on why they hold an opinion, and the consideration of the possibility that their opinion requires further evaluation.

Evaluating Other Opinions

To ensure that this type of examination occurs, Opposing Viewpoints books present all types of opinions. Prominent spokespeople on different sides of each issue as well as well-known professionals from many disciplines challenge the reader. An additional goal of the series is to provide a forum for other, less known, or even unpopular viewpoints. The opinion of an ordinary person who has had to make the decision to cut off life support from a terminally ill relative, for example, may be just as valuable and provide just as much insight as a medical ethicist's professional opinion. The editors have two additional purposes in including these less known views. One, the editors encourage readers to respect others' opinions—even when not enhanced by professional credibility. It is only by reading or listening to and objectively evaluating others' ideas that one can determine whether they are worthy of consideration. Two, the inclusion of such viewpoints encourages the important critical thinking skill of objectively evaluating an author's credentials and bias. This evaluation will illuminate an author's reasons for taking a particular stance on an issue and will aid in readers' evaluation of the author's ideas.

It is our hope that these books will give readers a deeper understanding of the issues debated and an appreciation of the complexity of even seemingly simple issues when good and honest people disagree. This awareness is particularly important in a democratic society such as ours in which people enter into public debate to determine the common good. Those with whom one disagrees should not be regarded as enemies but rather as people whose views deserve careful examination and may shed light on one's own.

Thomas Jefferson once said that "difference of opinion leads to inquiry, and inquiry to truth." Jefferson, a broadly educated man, argued that "if a nation expects to be ignorant and free . . . it expects what never was and never will be." As individuals and as a nation, it is imperative that we consider the opinions of others and examine them with skill and discernment. The Opposing Viewpoints Series is intended to help readers achieve this goal.

David L. Bender and Bruno Leone,
Founders

Greenhaven Press anthologies primarily consist of previously published material taken from a variety of sources, including periodicals, books, scholarly journals, newspapers, government documents, and position papers from private and public organizations. These original sources are often edited for length and to ensure their accessibility for a young adult audience. The anthology editors also change the original titles of these works in order to clearly present the main thesis of each viewpoint and to explicitly indicate the opinion presented in the viewpoint. These alterations are made in consideration of both the reading and comprehension levels of a young adult audience. Every effort is made to ensure that Greenhaven Press accurately reflects the original intent of the authors included in this anthology.

Introduction

"It has become almost axiomatic that the great rights which are secured for all of us by the Bill of Rights are constantly tested and retested in the courts by the people who live in the bottom of society's barrel."

—*Anthony Lewis,* Gideon's Trumpet, *1964*

One of the greatest challenges facing the criminal justice system is the need to balance the rights of accused criminals against society's interest in imposing punishments on those convicted of crimes. This tension is illustrated by the debate over whether defendants have the right to be represented by an attorney.

Most Americans are familiar with the *Miranda* warning, which advises suspects of their rights that are guaranteed by the Fifth and Sixth Amendments: Criminal suspects have the right to refuse to answer questions from police; they have the right to an attorney; and if they cannot afford an attorney, one will be provided for them at no charge. However, the right to a court-appointed attorney is relatively new. The federal government started providing court-appointed attorneys for felony defendants in the nineteenth century, and some states began appointing lawyers for indigent felony defendants in the early twentieth century. But in 1963, the U.S. Supreme Court ruled that an attorney must be provided to all criminal defendants in state and federal cases. The case that changed American jurisprudence was *Gideon v. Wainwright.*

Clarence Earl Gideon was a homeless ex-convict with an eighth-grade education. He was arrested in 1961 in Panama City for breaking and entering into a pool hall, a felony under Florida law. At his trial, he asked the court to appoint him a lawyer, but the judge in his case ruled that state law only allowed court-appointed attorneys for capital offenses. Gideon was therefore forced to represent himself during his trial, and not surprisingly, he was convicted by a jury and sentenced to five years in a state penitentiary. While in prison, Gideon wrote a letter to the U.S. Supreme Court asking the Court to review his case, and the Court decided to settle the question of who was entitled to have a court-appointed lawyer. In *Gideon*, the court ruled that a defendant's right to a fair trial should not depend on his or her wealth or education:

> In our adversary system of criminal justice, any person haled into court, who is too poor to hire a lawyer, cannot be assured a fair trial unless counsel is provided for him. This seems to us to be an obvious truth. . . . Lawyers in criminal courts are necessities, not luxuries.

The Supreme Court overturned Gideon's conviction and ordered a new trial. At his second trial, Gideon was provided with a lawyer who obtained an acquittal for him. States are now required to provide attorneys for all criminal defendants.

It is left up to the states to determine how they will provide legal counsel for indigent defendants, however. Some states have established a public defender's office, in which lawyers are paid by the state to defend poor defendants. Other states appoint a lawyer to act as the defendant's lawyer from a pool of available attorneys. These lawyers may work on a *pro bono* basis (meaning they work without pay for the public good), or they may bill the state for their services. Still other lawyers work on a contract basis with the state, agreeing to take on indigent defense cases for a specified fee.

It has been well-documented that a few attorneys appointed to represent indigent defendants have been inexperienced, poorly trained, and have even fallen asleep during their clients' trials. According to some Americans, these defendants are not experiencing a travesty of justice but—because they are guilty of the crime which they are accused of—are getting exactly what they deserve. Some critics even go so far as to suggest that the Supreme Court's ruling in *Gideon v. Wainwright* is wrong. Don Stott, a free-lance writer, argues:

> The Sixth Amendment to the Constitution says that, "In a criminal prosecution, the accused shall . . . have the assistance of counsel for his defense." It does not say that the state shall pay for such, or that "counsel" shall be a college-educated lawyer. It says the accused shall have the counsel *assist* in their defense . . . not perform it.

Others believe that taxpayer dollars should not be used to pay for defense lawyers. These opponents maintain that defendants should be provided with the minimum assistance required by law. When high-profile, experienced lawyers are allowed to defend the accused at government expense, critics contend that taxpayers are essentially paying to let guilty criminals escape punishment.

Supporters of public-supported defense attorneys maintain, however, that providing indigent criminal defendants with the best possible lawyers and defense is essential to upholding the integrity of the American criminal justice system. According to John Wasowicz, a lawyer in Virginia, if indigent defendants are represented by incompetent attorneys, "people would be able to say that there are two kinds of justice: one for people with money, and one for those who don't have the financial resources to mount a strong defense." Furthermore, he asserts, the core belief of American jurisprudence is that the accused is innocent until proven guilty, and so all defendants are entitled to a rigorous defense. Providing indigent defendants with a competent defense lawyer helps to ensure that innocent persons will be acquitted. Permitting or even encouraging incompetent lawyers to represent poor defendants increases the likelihood that an innocent person will be convicted and imprisoned. It also increases the possibility that the conviction will be reversed on appeal based on the grounds of ineffective assistance of counsel. Supporters also point out that if the defendant is found guilty, despite the best efforts of a competent defense lawyer, then it is less likely that an appeals court will find that an error has been made in the case and overturn the conviction. And a competent lawyer may be able to persuade the defendant to accept a plea bargain if the evidence against him or her is overwhelming. Wasowicz concludes, "Good court-appointed counsel does not jeopardize justice; it enhances it."

Whether or not those accused of a crime should be vigorously defended by lawyers, and whether lawyers should even accept such a case in the first place goes to the heart of the issues in *Criminal Justice: Opposing Viewpoints.* The authors examine these topics and others in the following chapters: Does the Criminal Justice System Need Reform? Is the Prison System Effective? Should Sentencing Laws Be Reformed? What Rights Should Be a Part of the Criminal Justice System? As long as people continue to commit crimes, questions will remain about how to prosecute, sentence, and imprison them.

Chapter 1

Does the Criminal Justice System Need Reform?

Chapter Preface

One of the most persistent complaints about the American criminal justice system is that the system and sometimes the people who work in it discriminate against blacks and other minorities, including the poor. Those who advocate reforming the criminal justice system contend that police use "racial profiling" to stop and harass minority drivers in the hope of finding a criminal offense. The American Civil Liberties Union unveiled an advertisement in late 2001 in an attempt to raise awareness of racial profiling. The ad featured Elmo Randolph, an African-American dentist who was stopped by New Jersey police more than one hundred times in a five-year period and yet never received a ticket. Randolph said of his experience, "The police searched my car and I had to prove to the troopers that being an African-American man in a nice car doesn't mean that I am a drug dealer or car thief."

Many criminal justice experts defend police traffic stops based on racial profiling. Journalist Heather MacDonald writes that state troopers have discovered, based on their experience, that "minorities were carrying most of the drugs" and also money or guns into and out of major cities such as New York City. According to MacDonald, while blacks make up only 13.5 percent of the population in New Jersey, they make up more than 60 percent of the arrests for drugs and weapons. Therefore, she concludes that stopping a motorist who fits the drug courier profile makes sense.

The question of whether the American criminal justice system is racist will probably never be settled to everyone's satisfaction. The authors in the following chapter examine this and other issues that are at the center of the debate over whether the criminal justice system needs to be reformed.

1 Viewpoint

"The federal grand jury today functions primarily as a tool of the federal prosecutor."

The Grand Jury System Needs Reform

Commission to Reform the Federal Grand Jury

The Commission to Reform the Federal Grand Jury is comprised of prosecutors, defense lawyers, and law professors who studied the federal grand jury system for two years before making its report. The commission asserts that the federal grand jury has changed from being an investigative body designed to be a safeguard against government zeal to one that is a rubber stamp for prosecutors. In order to once again protect American citizens from prosecutorial misconduct, the commission recommends that lawyers be allowed to accompany their clients and consult with them behind the closed doors of the jury chamber. Several states allow attorneys to consult with their clients in the grand jury room with no adverse effects, and this right should be extended to those being questioned by a federal grand jury.

As you read, consider the following questions:

1. What was the primary role of the grand jury when it was first incorporated into the Constitution, according to the commission?
2. As stated by the commission, what are three objections to allowing witnesses to have counsel in the grand jury room?
3. What is the commission's response to charges that permitting counsel in the grand jury room will lead to breaches of secrecy?

Commission to Reform the Federal Grand Jury, "Report of Commission to Reform the Federal Grand Jury," www.nacdl.org, May 18, 2000.

In 1791, when the grand jury was incorporated into our constitutional structure, its primary role was to protect the individual from unfounded accusations. As one observer [David L. Fine] has noted, "the grand jury had achieved renown as a bulwark against despotism, a protector of the common man against oppressive prosecution. The institution's investigatory role was secondary." But, in the subsequent 200 years, in the federal system anyway, "the protective function has been trivialized and the investigator's function expanded to the point where the institution is almost precisely the opposite of what the Founding Fathers intended."

Today, many would agree with the observation of William J. Campbell, former federal district judge in Chicago: "[T]oday, the grand jury is the total captive of the prosecutor who, if he is candid, will concede that he can indict anybody, at any time, for almost anything, before any grand jury."

What this means is that the federal grand jury is a secret ex parte proceeding where the evidence is presented by the prosecutor and the grand jury votes whether to indict without ever hearing from the court (other than a preliminary session welcoming the grand jurors and giving some general guidelines about their duties) or defense counsel. Unsurprisingly, under these circumstances the grand jurors tend to bond with the prosecutor and indict when the prosecutor indicates there should be an indictment.

A Tool of the Prosecutor

Thus, the federal grand jury today functions primarily as a tool of the federal prosecutor. Employing the power of compulsory process in a secret proceeding, the prosecutor investigates and determines, with virtually no check, who will be indicted and for what.

In the federal grand jury, the prosecutor exercises this enormous power unrestrained by law or judicial supervision. The grand jury process is largely devoid of legal rules. The prosecutor can present the evidence he or she wants to present in the manner he or she wants to present it. The only theoretical restriction is that, if an indictment is rendered, the evidence should be sufficient to establish probable cause that the accused committed the crime charged. Even that minimal test, however, finds no mechanism in the federal system for its enforcement. Any claimed insufficiency, unfairness or abuse in the grand jury proceedings is said to "merge" in the trial—prejudice from grand jury impropriety is deemed "cured" by a fair trial. But *an indictment alone* can cause enormous harm to an individual or business accused.

The result is a federal grand jury process virtually immune from judicial supervision. Because grand jury procedure presently is given little legal significance, federal courts engage in little scrutiny of what happens there. While some prosecutors may conduct grand jury proceedings with meticulous care and concern for fairness to targets, others may not. If abuses do occur, they will rarely come to light. . . .

The following ten reforms—a Bill of Rights for the Federal Grand Jury—are mainly drawn from those proposed by the American Bar Association (ABA) more than 20 years ago by its Criminal Justice Section Committee on the Grand Jury ("ABA Report"). Congress held hearings on these proposals but failed to pass them. However, recent developments, noted above, have created a new urgency to grand jury reform, as a critical policy step toward re-establishing a sense of fair balance to the now truly enormous federal prosecutorial/investigative power. . . .

Criticisms of Federal Grand Jury Reform Proposals

The critique of our grand jury reform proposals is largely encapsulated in opposition to the right to counsel in the grand jury room. First, opponents claim that the presence of counsel will transform the grand jury proceeding into an adversarial situation. This runs counter to the historic function of the grand jury and turns it, in effect, into another trial. Second, opponents argue that such reform will make the system of justice less efficient by encumbering the process with additional procedures.

These concerns mirror the critiques of other federal grand jury reform proposals. For example, the U.S. Supreme Court in the *United States vs. Calandra* case of the early 1970s, stated:

> Permitting witnesses to invoke the exclusionary rule before a grand jury would precipitate adjudication of issues hitherto

reserved for the trial on the merits and would delay and disrupt grand jury proceedings. Suppression hearings would halt the orderly progress of an investigation and might necessitate extended litigation of issues only tangentially related to the grand jury's primary objective. The probable result would be "protracted interruption of grand jury proceedings," effectively transforming them into preliminary trials on the merits. In some cases the delay might be fatal to the enforcement of criminal law.

Fear of delay and of turning federal grand jury proceedings into a "preliminary trial" are both cited as reasons for not extending the exclusionary rule to grand jury proceedings.

A third objection raised against counsel in the grand jury room is that it allows for the control of witnesses in corporate and organized crime cases, and high-level drug cases. The fear is that the subject of the investigation would control the selection of counsel for the witnesses, and that the witnesses' testimony would be less forthcoming with such counsel in the grand jury room.

Response to Criticisms

We think the critics fail to adequately appreciate the positive practical experiences of states which have implemented a number of these same reforms. Particularly notable in this respect are Colorado and New York.

In Colorado, for example, if a *Miranda*-like warning is not given to a witness before testimony, the witness cannot be prosecuted as a result of any information presented to the state grand jury. The warning includes an advisory as to the right to counsel. Defense counsel are allowed in the grand jury, but can only act as advisors, as would be the case under our proposal. According to H. Jeffrey Bayles, a former Denver chief deputy district attorney, the presence of counsel has not disrupted or impeded the functions of the grand jury. In fact, the opposite has been true. He explains:

> The presence of counsel has a definitely positive effect. Prosecutors who have worked under both the new and old laws strongly prefer the new. Not only does the new law speed the process by eliminating the walk outside the room on every question, but it also reduces the number of questions requiring conferences. The educational process, which of necessity accompanies having counsel in the grand jury

> room, promotes a better understanding of the grand jury within the bar. The more the processes are known, the less is the aura of mystery surrounding the grand jury. When the mystery leaves, so does much of the fear and distrust of the institution. The demand for abolition of the grand jury will decrease in direct proportion to the number of counsel who attend grand jury sessions with their clients.

Experiences in other states where counsel is permitted in the grand jury room appear to have been similarly successful.

The state grand jury in New York is also similar in many respects to the model we suggest. There, the rules of evidence for grand jury proceedings are virtually identical to those which govern trials. Targets have the right to testify on their own behalf and can recommend specific witnesses to the grand jury. Examination of reported decisions in New York, as well as the collective experience of Commission members from New York, reveals that procedures there have not led to the kind of inefficient mini-trials hypothesized by opponents of reform.

With respect to the claim that the proposal will allow control of witnesses in organized crime and drug cases, the case has not been made by critics of reform that state experiences have demonstrated that lawyers for witnesses have suborned perjury or obstructed the witness's truthful and complete grand jury testimony.

The reform proposal of permitting counsel for witnesses in the grand jury room certainly should not be rejected on the basis of what is, at best, a speculative claim. Further, should any such obstructionism actually emerge in any case, our proposal has made provision for its prompt and forceful correction by the supervising court. Our proposal is plain that the federal court with jurisdiction over the relevant grand jury shall enjoy a specific *congressionally-authorized* power (that is, not the inherent judicial power rejected by the *Williams* Court)—to remove, or otherwise sanction, an obstructionist lawyer.

To the extent that some critics express concern about witness counsel in the grand jury lending itself to increased breaches of secrecy by "house counsel" to a business or organized crime organization, this can also be addressed through the courts' attorney removal and other sanctioning powers. Moreover, realistically, in-house counsel can get this information anyway, albeit perhaps a *less-than-entirely-accurate* rendition. This is true of the objection to allowing witnesses access to the transcripts of their testimony, as well. Any potential for these reforms to increase breaches of secrecy is not an appreciable risk. As Watergate prosecutor, now White House Counsel, Charles Ruff has well explained:

> In the typical grand jury investigation into the activities of any hierarchically structured organization, a witness from the lower or middle levels represented by counsel hired by his superiors [the entity], will meet with the prosecutor and there will be some discussion both about his status and about the nature of his prospective testimony. If his lawyer advises him to assert his privilege against self-incrimination, and the prosecutor does not immunize him, it is difficult to see what added harm is created by permitting the witness' lawyer to be in the grand jury room. If the witness is advised to testify without asserting his privilege, there is some risk that he will be less candid if his employer's representative is present, but I question whether the risk is measurably greater than it is with the lawyer outside the grand jury room, since, if the witness' testimony is helpful to the government, that fact will probably become evident to the lawyer in fairly short order. If the government decides to immunize the witness, it has already announced that it considers him a potential witness against his employer, and has laid a firm basis for the [judicial] disqualification of [house] counsel.

Nor will our other proposed reforms disrupt the grand jury proceedings. Our proposals would not shift suppression and/or dismissal hearings back to the grand jury stage of proceedings. Rather, any suppression or dismissal motion would be made as one of several post-indictment, but pretrial, matters.

The Supreme Court has not spoken against the policy changes we advocate. True, in the early 1970s, in *United States v. Calandra*, the Supreme Court ruled that the *judicially created exclusionary rule* does not apply in grand jury proceedings. However, neither *Calandra* nor any other Supreme Court decision regarding the courts' limited *inherent* powers to address grand jury impropriety by prosecutors addresses the policy decision, exclusively reserved to Congress, as to the advisability of re-calibrated, statutory safeguards for the individual or business called before the modern federal grand jury.

Evidence illegally obtained by *electronic surveillance* is, in fact, specifically excluded by statute from use in the federal grand jury. In 1974, the *Calandra* Court felt it could confidently state that, "for the most part, a prosecutor would be unlikely to request an indictment where a conviction would not be obtained." Today, however, in the wake of a recent explosion in the number of federal prosecutors—with the accompanying "problems of quality control" identified by conservative jurists like Richard Posner and Alex Kozinski, among many others—that sort of confidence is called into serious question. With approximately four times the number of federal prosecutors, exercising vastly expanded powers over the citizenry in investigation and prosecution of manifold more federal criminal offenses, this belief is highly debatable. At least now, sound policy dictates that there simply should be no basis for a prosecutor to *even consider* utilizing in the grand jury evidence he or she believes to be unlawfully obtained.

If the federal grand jury is to serve its historical function of being shield as well as sword, the integrity of the process must be maintained. The fact that the Supreme Court has decided it does not possess the *inherent power* to supervise the federal grand jury is no argument against legislation excluding unconstitutionally obtained evidence from the process. In order to actually effectuate this sound principle, the federal courts must be congressionally empowered to dismiss, with or without prejudice, an indictment obtained through the grand jury in violation of this basic rule.

Compelling Need for Federal Grand Jury Reform

The purpose of federal grand jury reform is to bring about changes in the institution so that it might again function as most feel it should—as an investigative arm of the government capable of combating crime, but also, simultaneously, a critical protector of citizens' rights. Some, following certain court precedent, may object in the belief that the federal grand jury has never ceased to act as both a sword and shield. Some federal prosecutors may perceive such reforms as a threat to their ability to obtain indictments. But maintaining the *status quo* ignores the fundamental principles that are at the heart of our justice system in America.

The Grand Jury's Role Is Changing

The U.S. Constitution provides for grand juries as a right of the accused. If a grand jury is to be just a rubber stamp for a prosecutor, it would not be much of a right, and would not have commanded placement in the Bill of Rights, whose Fifth Amendment begins, "No person shall be held to answer for a capital, or otherwise infamous crime, unless on a presentment or indictment of a Grand Jury. . . ." This means that the grand jury is to function as a "check" upon the government, because by definition, the government is always the prosecutor in a criminal case. Most states which still honor the U.S. Constitution by using grand juries define a grand jury as a body of persons summoned by the sheriff to each session of the criminal courts, whose duty is to determine whether there is sufficient reason (that is, probable cause) to find a bill of indictment or presentment against a named individual or other entity. Present practice in many jurisdictions has been to shift grand juries from being a body sitting in judgment of the prosecution, to becoming the government's tool of inquisition. If unchallenged, a prosecutor can use the modern grand jury as a cover to gain power that the Constitution withholds from them (such as forcing people to testify against their will). This "modern" thing that they call a grand jury is not the grand jury contemplated in our Constitution.

Fully Informed Jury Association, "Frequently Asked Questions," no date.

Despite the increasingly compelling need for reform, the federal grand jury has remained largely unchanged. Two decades ago, at the urging of the American Bar Association and many others, Congress actively considered similar reform proposals. Numerous bills were introduced, detailed studies performed, and a multitude of testimony presented. Yet few changes resulted. Changes that did result—the recording of grand jury proceedings and issuance of prosecutorial guidelines—although helpful, have proved over the course of the intervening years to have very little impact on the core concerns that fueled the calls for modest reforms.

In the intervening decades, the number of federal prosecutors has exploded while effective controls against federal grand jury abuses have dwindled. The result has been an increase in prosecutorial excesses that has resulted in witness abuse and indictments that should never have been brought—destroying the lives, careers and businesses of innocent Americans. The need for federal grand jury reform, to safeguard the citizenry against such excess, has only gotten greater.

The federal grand jury is back in the spotlight. One can hardly open a newspaper or turn on the radio or television without hearing criticism or concerns about unfairness to citizens exposed to the grand jury process. Americans are troubled as their fellow citizens increasingly relate grueling and costly experiences as they emerge from testifying before a federal grand jury.

Rather than repeat the mistakes of the past, we need to learn from them. At the very least, if the case was not made in the 1970s for some basic federal grand jury reforms, we submit that recent experience has made the case for reform today. The modest measures recommended in this Report will help return the institution of the federal grand jury to its rightful place within our justice system—as a viable means for helping to ferret out criminal activity *while also ensuring fairness to all individuals and businesses who come within its focus.*

Federal Grand Jury Bill of Rights

1. A witness before the grand jury who has not received immunity shall have the right to be accompanied by counsel in his or her appearance before the grand jury. Such counsel shall be allowed to be present in the grand jury room only during the questioning of the witness and shall be allowed to advise the witness. Such counsel shall not be permitted to address the grand jurors, stop the proceedings, object to questions, stop the witness from answering a question, nor otherwise take an active part in proceedings before the grand jury. The court shall have the power to remove from the grand jury room, or otherwise sanction counsel for conduct inconsistent with this principle. . . .

2. No prosecutor shall knowingly fail to disclose to the federal grand jury evidence in the prosecutor's possession which exonerates the target or subject of the offense. Such disclosure obligations shall not include an obligation to dis-

close matters that affect credibility such as prior inconsistent statements. . . .

3. The prosecutor shall not present to the federal grand jury evidence which he or she knows to be constitutionally inadmissible at trial *because of a court ruling on the matter.* . . .

4. A target or subject of a grand jury investigation shall have the right to testify before the grand jury. Prosecutors shall notify such targets or subjects of their opportunity to testify, unless notification may result in flight, endanger other persons or obstruct justice, or unless the prosecutor is unable to notify said persons with reasonable diligence. A target or subject of the grand jury may also submit to the court, to be made available to the foreperson, an offer, in writing, to provide information or evidence to the grand jury. . . .

5. Witnesses should have the right to receive a transcript of their federal grand jury testimony. . . .

6. The federal grand jury shall not name a person in an indictment as an unindicted co-conspirator to a criminal conspiracy. Nothing herein shall prevent the prosecutor from supplying such names in a bill of particulars. . . .

7. All non-immunized *subjects or targets* called before a federal grand jury shall be given a *Miranda* warning by the prosecutor before being questioned. . . .

8. All subpoenas for witnesses called before a federal grand jury shall be issued at least 72 hours before the date of appearance, not to include weekends and holidays, unless good cause is shown for *an exemption*. . . .

9. The federal grand jurors shall be given meaningful jury instructions, on the record, regarding their duties and powers as grand jurors, and the charges they are to consider. All instructions, recommendations and commentary to grand jurors by the prosecution shall be recorded and shall be made available to the accused after an indictment, during pre-trial discovery, and the court shall have discretion to dismiss an indictment, with or without prejudice, in the event of prosecutorial impropriety reflected in the transcript. . . .

10. No prosecutor shall call before the federal grand jury any subject or target who has stated personally or through his attorney that he intends to invoke the constitutional privilege against self-incrimination.

2

VIEWPOINT

"Allowing witness counsel to accompany a witness to a grand jury proceeding, would, as a practical matter, destroy the effectiveness of our federal grand jury system."

The Grand Jury System Does Not Need Reform

James K. Robinson

Federal grand juries conduct their investigations of criminal wrong-doing in secret. James K. Robinson argues in the following viewpoint that permitting lawyers to accompany their clients into the grand jury room would disrupt and destroy the effectiveness of the grand jury's investigation. In addition, the presence of counsel in the chambers would transform the proceedings from a criminal investigation into a trial determining guilt or innocence. Finally, Robinson contends that allowing defense lawyers in the grand jury room would compromise the secrecy of the proceedings. Robinson is an assistant attorney general for the U.S. Department of Justice Criminal Division.

As you read, consider the following questions:

1. In Robinson's opinion, how would the presence of a defense lawyer in the grand jury room change the proceedings from an investigative tool to an adversarial trial to determine guilt or innocence?
2. How might counsel disrupt grand jury proceedings, according to the author?

James K. Robinson, "Constitutional Rights and the Grand Jury: Hearing before the Subcommittee on the Constitution of the Committee on the Judiciary, House of Representatives, 160th Congress, 2nd Session, July 27, 2000," http://commdocs.house.gov, July 2000.

Our grand jury system has changed very little over the last two hundred years because it works: it protects our citizens from crime and it protects the rights of the accused. There have, nonetheless, been intermittent calls for reform of the grand jury system. Most recently, the National Association of Criminal Defense Lawyers (NACDL) has announced its support for legislation to dramatically overhaul the operations of our federal grand jury system. . . .

Proposal: Allow counsel to accompany and advise his or her client inside the grand jury room.

It has long been the prevailing practice that counsel may not accompany the witness inside the grand jury room. The proposal to allow defense counsel to be permitted inside the grand jury room has been considered—and rejected—by previous Congresses. Proponents of this change argue that counsel is necessary to protect the witness's rights and to deter prosecutorial abuse. The grand jury is not a part of the adversarial criminal justice process. It is solely a screening tool to determine whether there is an adequate basis for bringing a criminal charge. We believe that allowing witness counsel to accompany a witness to a grand jury proceeding, would, as a practical matter, destroy the effectiveness of our federal grand jury system.

Reasons Against Counsel

First, the presence of an attorney in the grand jury room would interfere with the basic function of the grand jury—to thoroughly investigate allegations of violations of federal criminal law. The entire purpose of calling witnesses before the grand jury is to elicit whatever pertinent facts the witness knows. It is essential that witnesses provide truthful, full, unfettered and unsuggested testimony. If counsel were present, the witness might simply look to him or her for guidance on how to respond. A witness may be more likely to repeat the words his attorney whispered to him or her, rather than provide truthful and exhaustive testimony in his or her own words.

Second, the presence of counsel for the witness has the potential to change the federal grand jury from a body that investigates and charges federal crimes into one that determines guilt or innocence—and the process from an informal back and forth discussion to an adversarial proceeding. It is not the role of witness counsel to assist the grand jury in its search for truth. Rather, counsel has the responsibility to zealously represent his or her client and protect interests that are often inconsistent with the role of the grand jury. In particular, to the extent that a complete and truthful answer would arguably prejudice the witness in any way, counsel for the witness would not want his or her client to answer. Counsel would likely object to questions he or she regards as irrelevant, overbroad, or technically defective—objections that have historically had no place in grand jury investigations. With counsel present, these proceedings would devolve to arguments about evidentiary issues and other procedural concerns that have no place in the grand jury. Grand jurors themselves regularly pose questions to witnesses. These questions would undoubtedly fail to comport with technical requirements of guilt-determining proceedings; repeated objections by counsel would both disrupt the proceedings and chill grand jurors from making inquiries.

Some counsel might go further than representing a client and attempt to disrupt the proceeding itself. If counsel were present in the grand jury room without the presence of a judge, there would be the potential for some counsel to make frivolous objections, confer with their clients in stage whispers, refer to prejudicial material and otherwise act to impede the proceedings. We doubt that the restrictions on counsel proposed by the NACDL would prevent this disruptive behavior. Even with strict rules, counsel could still communicate through his or her client and disrupt the proceedings. At the same time, we are also deeply skeptical that adequate remedies exist to control disruptive counsel. Some have suggested that the offending counsel could be excluded from the grand jury room. We believe—and the Judicial Conference has stated—that courts would rightly be extremely reluctant to interfere in the attorney/client relationship by ordering that a witness's counsel be removed. In addition, there may be a substantial constitutional difficulty with ordering a witness to obtain other counsel against his wishes. The Judicial Conference has also voiced its concern that attorneys would not abide by the rules. In its 1999 report, the Conference adopted the following comment by a group of Second Circuit judges: "[e]xperience in criminal trials demonstrates that many lawyers simply would not adhere to the idealistic conception that they would limit themselves to advising their clients in sotto voce."

Court Delays

Third, the problems associated with the presence of counsel in the grand jury would result in repeated court intervention—and thus in significant delays and use of court resources. Every disagreement between a prosecutor and a witness' counsel would require an appearance before a judge who could control counsel only through the court's contempt powers. This would spawn protracted—and costly—litigation and lengthy delays. The grand jury must be free to act expeditiously to investigate crimes.

Delays that may be acceptable in other contexts are uniquely damaging in the grand jury system. Although limited extensions can be obtained with court approval, grand jury proceedings are limited to eighteen months. In our many complex cases, such as organized crime, terrorism and white collar crime, the grand jury needs its full tenure to adequately conduct its investigative and charging functions. The inevitable inclination of witnesses to consult their attorneys before every question would render the proceedings sluggish. Coupled with the breaks to litigate disruptions by counsel, these delays would detract from the time allotted to the grand jury to complete its work.

Secrecy in Jeopardy

Fourth, the admission of counsel into the grand jury would place in jeopardy the secrecy that is so key to the effectiveness of the grand jury. Counsel, privy to the secret testimony presented in the grand jury room, could use this information to tailor the later testimony of other witnesses and thwart the investigation. Counsel could also discern the direction of the investigation and prepare later witnesses accordingly. This would certainly compromise the ability of the grand jury to elicit truthful, untainted testimony. It would also create an additional source for the release of secret information to the public. Like witnesses, counsel are not required to keep grand jury information confidential under Rule 6(e). Nothing would prevent counsel from sharing this information with the subjects, targets, prospective witnesses or the press. Counsel could use their access to make misleading comments that could influence future witnesses or trial jurors. Furthermore, having counsel in the grand jury room further complicates the investigation of grand jury leaks because it expands the universe of potential sources. Dissemination of such sensitive information at the grand jury stage would make the already difficult job of securing testimony from recalcitrant or reluctant witnesses more difficult and, in some cases, impossible. It could also encourage suspects to flee prior to an indictment.

Fifth, the presence of counsel in the grand jury room would make it difficult for a witness to testify candidly about his or her employer, business, union, organization or syndicate whose activities are under investigation. In many of our cases, these witnesses are represented by a "company lawyer." Individual witnesses who possess relevant information are often willing to cooperate in the investigation and provide testimony against their employers. However, this cooperation may be premised on the condition that their cooperation not become known—at least until trial—to the employer, fellow union members, or others who may cause them harm. If the attorney were present in the grand jury room, the witness would actually be unable to cooperate for fear of reprisal. The witness would not be able to decline the presence of counsel without tipping off the organization or syndicate to his cooperation. Furthermore, the witness could not realistically cooperate outside of the grand jury setting because the failure to be called in front of the grand jury would itself be noticeable. In these cases, permitting counsel in the grand jury room would have the ironic effect of paralyzing those witnesses willing to cooperate and chilling candid testimony.

Other Problems

Similar problems arise in cases of multiple representation—where one attorney, or a group of closely associated counsel, represent more than one grand jury witness. This is particularly common in investigations of organized criminal enterprises, business frauds, antitrust violations and other white collar offenses. Multiple representation creates the opportunity to thwart a legitimate investigation by obtaining valuable information from one client that can be used to advise other clients on how to tailor their responses in light of earlier testimony. This type of planning and fine-tuning of testimony can seriously mislead the grand jury and wholly undermine its work. In order to do tremendous damage to the

Comparing Grand and Petit Juries

Grand Jury	Petit (Trial) Jury
• 23 jurors, 16 must be present to run session	• 12 jurors (sometimes 6 or 8), all must be present
• No judge present	• Judge present
• Witnesses cannot have a lawyer present	• Witnesses can have a lawyer present
• 12 out of 23 jurors must vote to indict	• Decisions usually unanimous
• Closed, secret court	• Open court (except Juvenile)
• Do not have to present both sides	• Must present both sides
• Not all evidence needs to be presented	• All the evidence must be presented
• Conducted by the prosecutor	• Conducted by the judge
• Do not have to prove the evidence to be relevant	• Evidence has to be relevant
• Jurors serve for extended terms (Up to 36 months in the federal system)	• Jurors serve "one day/one trial"
• Witnesses must testify—accused does not	• Accused can plead the 5th amendment
• Jurors decide if there will be a trial	• Jurors decide guilt or innocence

Constitutional Rights Foundation Chicago, "The Grand Jury," no date.

grand jury's investigation, all counsel need to do is sit quietly during the proceeding and then use the information outside of the grand jury room.

Proponents of change have asserted that states that permit witness counsel in the grand jury room have not experienced these anticipated difficulties. Assuming for the sake of discussion that such assertions are true, as we stated earlier, the state experience is not a reliable predictor for federal proceedings. Most state prosecutors are not required to proceed through the grand jury and therefore states use grand juries infrequently. Also, there is a substantial difference in the nature of crimes prosecuted in the state and federal systems. While there are some states that regularly prosecute complex crimes, as a general matter, most state crimes do not necessitate the exhaustive use of the grand jury's investigative powers that federal cases require. Typically, the state caseload is dominated by cases that utilize government witnesses such as police officers. Because these witnesses work with the government, they will be unlikely to bring attorneys into the grand jury room or do anything to compromise the government's case. In contrast, the federal caseload includes organized crime, white collar crime, narcotics cases, environmental crimes, civil rights cases, and other complex matters in which the grand jury must sift through considerable evidence, hear from numerous witnesses—many of whom are hostile to the government's case—and determine who to charge. The types of dangers enumerated above are significantly more likely to occur in these cases.

Counsel Is Available

Finally, we should note that there is no discernible problem of unfairness or prosecutorial misconduct to rectify through the presence of counsel in the grand jury room. Today, every grand jury witness is free to consult with his or her counsel during grand jury proceedings. It is long-standing grand jury practice to permit the witness to step outside of the grand jury room to consult with counsel for any reason and at any time. Moreover, federal prosecutors routinely instruct grand jurors not to be prejudiced against a witness who exercises the right to consult with counsel. In addition, grand jury proceedings are recorded and judicial review of alleged prosecutorial misconduct is available. It is not necessary to have counsel monitor the proceedings in order to secure this information.

In short, the presence of counsel in the federal grand jury would certainly interfere with our ability to effectively charge and prosecute serious federal crimes and our ability to protect the public from dangerous felons. It would be a dangerous step for Congress to take and one that the Department opposes, as it has under both Democratic and Republican administrations for more than 20 years. . . .

The Last Line of Defense

Our federal criminal justice system is a model for criminal justice systems around the world. Today's grand jury is the effective sword and shield that it has been for hundreds of years. It is not a court of law. It is, and should remain, an investigative body of ordinary citizens tasked with the critical job of investigating complex and sensitive matters and deciding who should be prosecuted. It would be wrong today to try to turn this important investigative body into an adversarial tribunal and dangerous to leave our communities unprotected by unduly hindering federal law enforcement.

The Department of Justice is not alone in its concern about these proposals. The Judicial Conference of the United States, which speaks on behalf of the federal judges who are responsible for administering the grand jury system, has repeatedly rejected attempts to substantially depart from those practices which make our grand jury such an effective tool. In a report issued in 1975, and in another report issued in 1999, the Judicial Conference voiced its belief that the claimed misconduct of government attorneys is not so prevalent as to justify changes in practice. It also stated that current law, coupled with Department practice, contains more than adequate safeguards. We join the Judicial Conference in opposing reforms that would impair our ability to protect our communities.

We are fortunate in this country that over the past decade, crime has dropped each year and is now at its lowest level in a quarter of a century. But we cannot become complacent.

We cannot weaken those very systems that protect our nation from dangerous criminals. Keep in mind that we are dealing with people who threaten our national security, offend our civil rights, traffic in narcotics and sell drugs to our children, run organized crime syndicates, and pollute and hurt our environment. Often, the federal criminal justice system is the last line of defense for vulnerable communities and thus it needs to be as strong as possible. We must not erode those institutions that have served us for hundreds of years. There are many aspects of our justice system that badly need attention and we would urge you to focus on those areas that would truly benefit from legislative reform.

3

VIEWPOINT

"The short answer to the question of how can one defend a guilty client is that the client is not guilty until proven so and that until that time must receive zealous advocacy."

All Accused Criminals Are Entitled to a Robust Defense

Richard Hustad Miller

Richard Hustad Miller argues in the following viewpoint that providing a defendant with a vigorous defense is a crucial aspect of the criminal justice system. In response to critics who accuse lawyers of defending guilty clients, he insists that in the American criminal justice system the accused defendant is presumed innocent until proven guilty in a court of law. It is the prosecutor's responsibility to prove the defendant's guilt beyond a reasonable doubt, while the defense lawyer is required to provide a zealous defense using every legal means available. Miller is an attorney practicing in Connecticut.

As you read, consider the following questions:

1. What is the definition of a crime, according to the author?
2. Why is the criminal justice system an adversarial system, in the author's opinion?
3. When is justice best served by ignorance, according to Miller?

Criminal defense law is perhaps the most misunderstood practice in the profession of law. Perhaps the most misunderstood area within that practice is evidenced by the frequently asked question: "how can you defend a guilty person?" This essay attempts to answer that question by explaining how criminal defense law really works.

Most people understand the criminal defense lawyer according to character portrayals of the entertainment industry. According to the character Perry Mason, some believe the profession to be a continuously exciting field in which the attorney rapidly moves from case to case solving his client's problems with keen detective work and by uncovering the real guilty party. According to numerous other depictions, criminal defense lawyers are a deceitful group who have a pile of under-handed tricks that they use to get their client off on a technicality. Both are extremes that do not reflect reality. In fact, it is a well-regulated profession in which there is a well-established system virtually prohibiting surprise and high ethical standards demanding adherence to the system.

Criminal defense lawyers play only a single role in a well-established system designed to determine guilt or innocence. The legal system created by the United States Constitution and refined by legislative statutes and common law decisions establishes an adversarial method by which the government, represented by the judge, guides the people, represented by a jury, to a conclusion of whether the defendant has done something that is prohibited by the system.

Innocent Until Proven Guilty

The most important principle in this established system is that the defendant is innocent until proven guilty. Therefore, the short answer to the question of how can one defend a guilty client is that the client is not guilty until proven so and that until that time must receive zealous advocacy. This answer, however, is not sufficient because it leaves one with the belief that a criminal defense attorney uses procedure as a shield from any sense of justice.

While procedure alone is not controlling, justice comes only through the use of the system. The legal system is not necessarily a reflection of popular morality; it is positive law in which an act must be specifically prohibited in order for it to be considered a crime. Thus, the word 'crime' is a term of art meaning any act that is prohibited by the system. Justice is achieved only when a crime is proven and that happens only after the mechanisms of the system have operated.

Those expected to determine whether a crime has been committed are the people, represented by the jury. Their function is to determine guilt or innocence according to the law, not their own morality. There are a number of jurors, usually at least six, to guard against the application of private morality. And as a last resort, the judge can overrule a jury when s/he believes its verdict was contrary to the facts. The jury makes its decision based on the evidence presented and the arguments made by the opposing attorneys.

To ensure that the best prosecution and defense are presented to the jury, the system is adversarial, pitting the proponents of prosecution against those of defense. The purpose for this stems from an understanding of human nature: human beings cannot be entirely objective and using their subjectivity as an asset is better than attempting to overcome it. Thus, each opposing attorney is assigned responsibility for advocating only one side and is expected to use the natural tendencies of subjectivity to assert that side's point of view to the greatest possible extent. However, each side must conduct themselves according to the rules of the competitive system.

Legal Requirements

The system of advocating each side is governed by established rules and according to well-known legal requirements. There are no under-handed tricks available to either attorney. There are only established procedural rules detailing precisely how a trial is to be conducted and what defenses and mechanisms can be used. This is not to say there is only one way of doing things. To the contrary, there are many possible courses of actions, each one of which is a tactical decision. It is in this area that the better defense attorneys distinguish themselves. They are better not because they have devised some devilish trick or surprise attack, but because they know all the rules and all of the law and are very good at determining which course of action maximizes the defense position. A good attorney is so because s/he knows the system.

Deviation from the system of rules is not only prohibited, but strictly punished. An attorney who uses deceit or any other means of defense that is not lawful is subject to censure or even disbarment. The boards of ethics in the various states and federal districts take such deviations very seriously and issue punishments accordingly.

Defense Lawyer Ethics

"How does it make you feel when you have to compromise your ethics by defending guilty criminals?" This is a question I am asked at least once a week. I once asked a priest if he was ever asked the priestly analogue to that question: "How does it make you feel when you have to compromise your ethics by not disclosing crimes that penitents confide to you during confession?" He was shocked: "What do you mean, 'compromise my ethics'? That *is* my ethic—not to disclose what I have been told in the confessional." He stated indignantly that he had *never* been asked that question or anything like it.

Most thoughtful people don't accept the criminal defense lawyer's answer to the original question: "What do you mean, 'compromise my ethics'? That *is* my ethic—to defend people accused of crime, whether I believe that they may be innocent or guilty." If you can't deal with that, don't become a defense lawyer.

Alan Dershowitz, *Letters to a Young Lawyer*, 2001.

Likewise, poor attorney advocacy is prohibited, whether due to neglect or incompetence. An attorney must present a case thoroughly using all legal means of defense. This even includes refraining from defending a case to which the attorney lacks the necessary skills. This is especially so in the case of a criminal defense attorney whose client is in jeopardy of losing liberty or even life.

The Defense Attorney's Job

But what about if the defense attorney knows the client is guilty? The easy answer to this is that the defense attorney should never ask the client that question or allow the client to confess to him/her. It is not for the defense attorney to determine whether a crime was committed. To do so is a substitution of the values of the defense attorney in the place of the jury's determination of a legal conclusion and undermines the search for justice within the system. The more difficult answer is that the defense attorney should not concern him/herself with overtaking the job of the jury and passing judgment on the client. That not only is contrary to the role of the defense attorney, but interferes with the role that is expected of him/her. The most zealous advocacy of a client's position cannot be attained when the defense attorney is morally troubled in an attempt to judge a client. In this situation, justice is served by ignorance.

Therefore, the job of the criminal defense attorney is to present the most effective case possible in opposition to the prosecution. This is not only the defendant's right, but an essential part of the determination of justice. The jury needs to hear all sides thoroughly and completely before determining whether a crime has been committed. Anything short of that undermines the legitimacy of the system.

Finally, when one is disturbed by a trial verdict, it is not the defense attorney that should be blamed for using the tools provided to him/her by the system. If one does not like the tools, one should attempt to change them, not the person who utilizes them. Criminal defense is simply a profession that works within the system. Unfavorable criminal trial decisions are made by the people—the jurors—not the attorneys.

So when a person asks how can you defend the guilty, the answer is that only the people can decide if the defendant is guilty and until they have spoken, through the jury, the criminal defense attorney must use the tools created by the people, through the Congress, to properly represent an accused.

4

VIEWPOINT

"Nothing in the canons of ethics of the American Bar Association says a lawyer has to represent everyone who comes to his door."

Lawyers Are Not Obligated to Defend Guilty Clients

Vincent Bugliosi

Vincent Bugliosi is a prominent prosecuting attorney and author. In the following viewpoint, excerpted from his book *Outrage: The Five Reasons Why O.J. Simpson Got Away with Murder*, Bugliosi analyzes the murder trial of former football player O.J. Simpson. Bugliosi has no doubt that Simpson is guilty of the murders of his ex-wife and her companion, and for that reason he declares that he would never have agreed to defend Simpson during his trial. While Bugliosi fervently believes that every defendant has the right to an attorney, he asserts that there are so many lawyers available that it is completely ethical for him to represent only those clients he believes to be innocent or victims of mitigating circumstances.

As you read, consider the following questions:

1. Why does Bugliosi reject the argument that idealism motivates most defense attorneys when they represent guilty defendants?
2. In what circumstances would Bugliosi defend an obviously guilty client?
3. Why is the author critical of the way in which Simpson's lawyers defended him?

Vincent Bugliosi, *Outrage: The Five Reasons Why O.J. Simpson Got Away with Murder*. New York: W.W. Norton, 1996.

During my radio and television appearances on the O.J. Simpson case, I was frequently asked if I would have represented Simpson. Since I knew he was guilty, I always responded I would not have.

Idealism Versus Ambition

Some have been disturbed by my not wanting to represent anyone charged with murder or any violent crime unless I believe him or her to be innocent or unless there are substantially mitigating circumstances. Isn't everyone entitled to be represented by an attorney, guilty or innocent? In fact, that's the idealistic chant often recited by defense attorneys as justification for representing even the most vicious criminals in our society. The concept is unassailable, but idealism is rarely what motivates lawyers who represent guilty defendants. They take the work because trying cases is their livelihood, and they are ambitious to advance their careers. These motivations, while perfectly proper, are clearly not idealistic.

True idealism would be demonstrated in a hypothetical situation such as the following. Suppose a family is brutally murdered in a small town, and none of the five lawyers in town is willing to represent the suspect because the enraged citizens are all convinced of the suspect's guilt and no lawyer wants to be ostracized in the community for attempting to get the suspect off. Finally, one attorney steps forward and says, "I don't care what my friends at the Rotary Club and the First Baptist Church say. This is America, and everyone is entitled under the Sixth Amendment to our Constitution to be represented by an attorney."

That would be idealism. I, too, would represent a defendant—even one I believed to be guilty of murder—if I were the only lawyer available, because the right to counsel is a sacred right in our society and much more important than any personal predilection I might have. But this type of situation simply does not exist in a city like Los Angeles, where 35,000 lawyers stumble over each other's feet for cases. (For instance, when Charles Manson was charged with the Tate-LaBianca murders, over two hundred lawyers signed in to see him at the county jail, obviously for the purpose of seeking to represent him.) So I am free to follow my inclination.

Since nothing in the canons of ethics of the American Bar Association says a lawyer has to represent everyone who comes to his door, I choose not to defend anyone charged with a violent crime unless I believe he or she is innocent or unless there are substantially mitigating circumstances. (By the latter, I don't mean the question said to be asked about the victim by hard-bitten sheriffs in rural Texas at the start of any homicide investigation: "Did he *need* killing?") I investigate my own cases, and if I become satisfied in my own mind that the person is guilty, with no substantial mitigation, I routinely refer the case to other lawyers.

My Motivation

My position is not a matter of high ethics. It's more a matter of motivation. Let's take some vicious SOB who picks up young girls, sexually abuses and brutalizes them, then murders them and dumps them on the side of the road. What conceivable motivation could I possibly have to knock myself out working a hundred hours a week trying to figure out a way to get this type of person off?

I am also not unmindful of the fact that were I to secure a not-guilty verdict for one of these defendants I represented and he went out and did it again, I could rationalize all I wanted, but I would be partially responsible. If I had not deceived the jury the first time around, there would not have been a second murder.

In a nutshell, although I have never been a law-and-order fanatic—in fact, I'm suspicious of those who are—I do believe that those who have committed serious crimes should be severely punished, and I do not want to be in a position of actively seeking to thwart this natural justice.

The Jeffrey MacDonald Case

One illustration of my dilemma in legal defense work was the case of Dr. Jeffrey MacDonald, the Princeton-educated former U.S. Army Green Beret who was accused of savagely stabbing to death his pregnant wife and two young daughters in their Fort Bragg, North Carolina, home one rainy night in March 1970. He was first charged with the murders that year, but the case against him was dropped because the

Ninety-Five Percent Are Guilty

About 95 percent of all people charged with a crime end up guilty via plea bargaining. So by default, the overwhelming number of clients defense attorneys represent are found guilty of something.

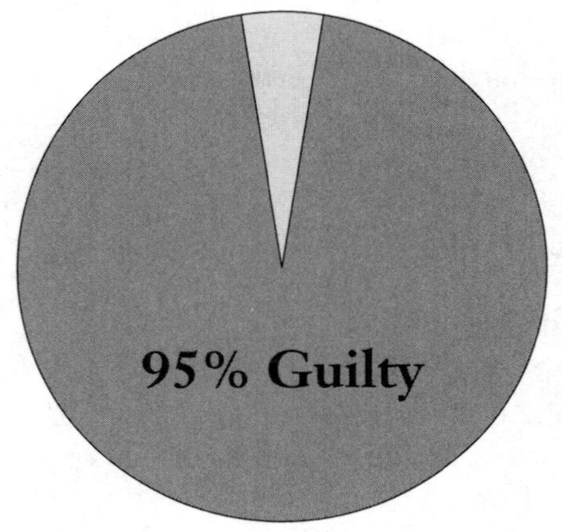

Timothy J. McClain, *San Diego Metro*, November 1996.

evidence was insufficient. It was sometime in late 1973 or early 1974 that a close woman friend of MacDonald's came to my office in Beverly Hills and told me that the doctor, who was then working as an emergency room physician in nearby Long Beach, had learned he was about to be reindicted. She said the doctor wanted to know if I would be interested in representing him. We could talk about it, I said, if the doctor was innocent. I told her, "Tell him, though, that for starters I want him to take and pass a polygraph test." While waiting to hear from him, I telephoned the federal prosecutor handling the case in North Carolina and asked what he had against MacDonald. The prosecutor would not say very much, but did mention a few pieces of evidence to me, one of which was that fibers from MacDonald's blue pajamas had been found embedded beneath the fingernails of his two-and-a-half-year-old daughter. That evoked in my mind the horrifying scene of a little girl crying out, "Daddy, Daddy, no," as she reached out and struggled against her father while he stabbed her to death. That was enough for me. I wanted nothing to do with the case. MacDonald's lady friend called a week later anyway to say that he did not think it was necessary to take a polygraph as a precondition to my representing him. Convicted of the triple murder in 1979, he was sentenced to three consecutive life terms in prison.

My disinclination to defend a murderer also resulted in my electing not to represent former San Francisco supervisor Dan White for the 1978 assassination murders of Mayor George Moscone and Supervisor Harvey Milk when friends of White's from the San Francisco Police Department—White was a former officer—asked me to.

Those are the only two really big murder defendants who have ever come to me. Since my image is still that of a prosecutor, when people get in trouble with the law, I'm usually one of the very last people they think of.

O.J. Simpson's Defense

Just because I could never have defended O.J. Simpson for these murders since I know he committed them does not mean I'm critical of the lawyers who did defend him for having done so. What I *am* very critical about is in *the way* several of them went about doing it. It's one thing to defend someone you know is guilty, even defend him vigorously. Who can validly criticize such a lawyer? Our system of justice and jurisprudence not only allows but encourages this.

But inasmuch as the defense lawyers had to know Simpson was guilty of these two terribly brutal murders, I personally wonder how they could possibly have found it within themselves to go far beyond a vigorous representation, defending him with the same passion and fervor with which one would defend his own parents, wife, or children who were being charged with a serious crime.

Moreover, although it's perfectly proper to defend a guilty person by trying to poke holes in the people's case, you don't, for instance, deliberately violate the rules, as Johnnie Cochran did when he argued throughout his opening statement (which is not allowed), and you don't, in your opening statement, refer to witnesses whose identity and statements have not been turned over to the prosecution (in violation of the law). More important, you don't (Cochran, F. Lee Bailey, Barry Scheck) accuse innocent police officers of framing your client for murder. You don't (Cochran, Bailey) inject the transparently fraudulent issue of race into the trial, particularly when it's to the detriment, as it was with Cochran, of your own race. You don't (Cochran and Scheck) object time and again during the prosecutors' final summations, in a concerted, unprofessional, and unethical effort to interrupt the flow of their arguments, therefore denying the people their right to a fair trial. . . .

To borrow a phrase from Henry Roth's recent novel, *From Bondage*, in the ensuing years each of the aforementioned defense attorneys in the Simpson case will have to "reconcile himself with himself." Unless, that is, as another novelist, Gertrude Stein, once said about Oakland, California, "there's no there, there."

VIEWPOINT

"To afford [terrorists], at the risk of our citizens' safety, the same due process applied to criminal defendants in the civilian justice system, is to extend to them rights that they do not have."

Terrorists Should Be Tried in a Military Tribunal

Neal A. Richardson and Spencer J. Crona

Neal A. Richardson is a deputy district attorney in Denver. Spencer J. Crona, a former newspaper editor and reporter, is a lawyer in Colorado. In the following viewpoint, they argue that terrorists are waging an illegal war by targeting civilians and noncombatants. Their actions make them illegal combatants, so they may be treated as spies or war criminals rather than prisoners of war. These enemies should be tried by military tribunals, which are more concerned with protecting national security than the terrorists' civil rights.

As you read, consider the following questions:

1. What makes an enemy an "illegal combatant," according to the U.S. Supreme Court?
2. According to the authors, who comprises a military commission?
3. Why do Richardson and Crona support a sure and swift death sentence for terrorists?

Neal A. Richardson and Spencer J. Crona, "Let Military Panels Punish Terrorists," *Los Angeles Times*, September 23, 2001, p. M7.

The prime objective in war should be the defeat of the enemy on the field of battle. But what if terrorist operatives are captured instead of killed? What if the good offices of our newfound friends the Pakistanis result in the delivery to our custody of Osama bin Laden himself? Must we spend millions of dollars and months for pretrial hearings, mega-trials [and] endless appeals as we furnish him the panoply of constitutional safeguards afforded ordinary defendants in our civilian system of criminal justice?

Illegal Combatants

The acts at issue here [the September 11, 2001, attacks] are far graver than acts of war. These have been acts of horrific violence directed deliberately and with premeditation toward civilians and noncombatants. Under the law of nations, such acts in war are "crimes against humanity." Further, directing attacks against military targets, like the destroyer *Cole* or the Pentagon, does not save the terrorist from being branded as a war criminal. According to Supreme Court precedent, enemies who wear no uniforms, hide their weapons from view and act as saboteurs are illegal combatants who may be executed as if they were spies rather than treated as prisoners of war.

When apprehended, such enemy infiltrators waging illegal war are not to be tried in the civilian courts, but before a military commission. This is neither an international tribunal based on the Nuremberg model nor a court-martial as in a nation's own armed forces, but rather a court composed of military officers designated to try and punish enemy combatants who are violating the laws of war. Such courts were used during and after World War II for Nazi saboteurs who landed on our eastern shore and in the trial of Gen. Tomoyuki Yamashita, who presided over Japanese soldiers' savage atrocities in the Philippines against civilians and prisoners of war. None of these offenders was able to avoid execution by appealing that he was denied the right to a civilian jury trial and the full due process protections of the civilian system of justice.

The military commission approach to bringing captured terrorists "to justice" presents distinct advantages. Unlike the war-crime tribunals in Europe for Balkan war atrocities, military commissions may apply the death penalty. Moreover, terrorist war criminals caught before they are able to commit mass murder—not just the successful ones—may be executed. This is significant, considering that the recent gang of terrorists committed suicide as part of their scheme. For them, there clearly was no moral difference between the plot and the completed act. Accordingly, the captured terrorist should not find refuge in an artificial distinction.

Don't Coddle Terrorists in Court

There is nothing wrong with [military] tribunals operating in public to enhance confidence in their outcomes, except when classified information needs to be safeguarded. But there is everything wrong with demanding an evidentiary standard of proof beyond a reasonable doubt. The late Supreme Court Justice William J. Brennan Jr. thought this standard necessary to ensure the liberty of individuals "going about ordinary affairs." But there is nothing ordinary about the destructive aims of terrorists. . . .

A standard of proof beyond reasonable doubt is hardly compatible with a proceeding for ferreting out a network of terrorist cells, expeditiously punishing terrorist ring leaders and preventing future attacks. It is especially unsuitable for a trial based on intelligence intercepts and informants who necessarily must operate with less substantiation. Nor does it make sense when witnesses are just as likely to be crossing the Pakistan border as hiding in a cave in Tora Bora.

Douglas W. Kmiec, *Los Angeles Times*, January 6, 2002.

Obviously the death penalty is no deterrent to people who believe that dying for their cause is martyrdom. But there are practical reasons for wanting swift and sure death sentences for terrorist war criminals. Before the recent plane hijackings, the history of modern terrorism was replete with examples of terrorists commandeering airplanes and ships. The objective of those terrorists was to hold hostages to exchange for the release of imprisoned comrades. If the imprisoned comrades have been executed, the value of taking hostages is diminished.

In the terrorism context, the whole question about the legality of assassination under an old executive order is a red herring. Now that we are engaged in at least the constitutional equivalent of a declared war, neutralizing the command and control structure of the enemy forces, including specific enemy personnel, is entirely legitimate. Should we not have specifically targeted and shot down Adm. Isoroku Yamamoto's plane during World War II? Should we not have assassinated Adolf Hitler, had the opportunity presented itself?

Other Advantages

Another advantage of the military system would be the opportunity for a proper military interrogation of the suspects. Do we want to give an arrested terrorist suspect, who could have the information to save the next 5,000 innocent lives, the Miranda warning to clam up and lawyer up?

Finally, the military commission would bypass the obstacle course of evidentiary rules that bogs down many criminal prosecutions. It would favor the admission of evidence instead of the exclusion based on how that evidence was obtained. Tapes of the cell phone calls of the doomed aboard the airliners, for example, would probably be admitted rather than possibly excluded as hearsay.

The military commission approach would err more on the side of protecting national security rather than the side of freeing the guilty to achieve absolute fairness in the process. Some will contend that this would institutionalize a transgression of civil liberties that, in effect, "lets the terrorist win" by depriving people of basic rights.

Such rhetoric misstates the law. The suspects we are talking about are foreign enemy agents, apprehended amid a declared state of war.

To afford such individuals, at the risk of our citizens' safety, the same due process applied to criminal defendants in the civilian justice system, is to extend to them rights that they do not have.

Viewpoint 6

"Convicting alleged terrorists in secret trials without the process due Americans . . . will hand Al Qaeda an enormous propaganda victory."

Terrorists Should Be Tried in the Criminal Justice System

Anne-Marie Slaughter

In the following viewpoint, Anne-Marie Slaughter argues against trying terrorists in military tribunals instead of in the civilian criminal justice system. Military tribunals violate the basic civil liberties that all Americans consider a part of their very identity. Slaughter also contends that convicting Islamic terrorists in secret without due process will alienate the same Muslims the United States is trying to win over. Furthermore, trying terrorists in a military court identifies them as soldiers when they are nothing more than global criminals. Slaughter is J. Sinclair Armstrong Professor of Law at Harvard Law School and president of the American Society of International Law.

As you read, consider the following questions:

1. In what ways do military tribunals differ from civilian criminal trials, according to Slaughter?
2. How does the war on terror differ from other wars, in the author's opinion?
3. In Slaughter's view, what is the best way to fight the war on terror?

Anne-Marie Slaughter, "Terrorists on Trial," *Commonweal*, vol. 128, December 7, 2001, p. 8.

In his first speech to the American people after September 11, 2001, President George W. Bush said "we will bring the terrorists to justice or justice to the terrorists." In mid-November 2001, the administration clarified what it meant by bringing justice to the terrorists—trial by military tribunal. Under rules drafted by the Pentagon, such tribunals are not subject to constitutional safeguards; they are without the normal burden of proof required in U.S. criminal trials; and they allow the possibility of presenting evidence in secret as well as admitting evidence that would not be admissible in U.S. trials. Judgment would be by two-thirds of the military judges appointed, without possibility of review by any civilian court. Convicted defendants would be subject to the death penalty.

Objections

Many individuals and institutions have already condemned this plan, ranging from the *New York Times* editorial board to conservative columnist William Safire. Most of these condemnations focus on the violations of civil liberties that Americans not only take for granted but also consider part of their birthright and their very identity as a people. The criticisms are well-placed and justified. Other objections concern the long-term impact on our ability to fight and win the war against terrorism. Convicting alleged terrorists in secret trials without the process due Americans, even American terrorists like Timothy McVeigh, will hand Al Qaeda an enormous propaganda victory and make it much more difficult to win hearts and minds across the Islamic world. Further, trial in military tribunals dignifies defendants as soldiers in an Islamic army, rather than treating them as the global criminals they are.

We are essentially fighting a particularly frightening and deadly form of global organized crime. Fighting organized crime at home poses many of the same difficulties: the tension between securing convictions and jeopardizing informants, security risks, the difficulty of actually getting sufficient evidence to convict. But we have developed laws and procedures that make it possible to hunt down and prosecute master criminals in global criminal networks of drug-runners, traffickers in women, illicit arms sales, and other dangerous activity. We can fight global terrorist networks the same way.

A Globetrotting Executioner

The sweep of the order [authorizing military tribunals to try suspected terrorists] is extraordinary. President George Bush has arrogated to himself the right to apprehend "any individual who is not a United States citizen" and subject that person to a secret military trial and then impose the death penalty. So, even if you're a legal immigrant, he can round you up, try you, and fry you. Plus, he can go anywhere around the world, nab any citizen of a foreign country, and drag that person into his kangaroo court, which he can hold "outside or within the United States." He thus can become a globetrotting executioner.

Progressive, January 2002.

But isn't this a war? Yes, in the sense that the threat posed by terrorist networks is sufficiently lethal to justify, at least under present circumstances, the limited use of armed force to pursue them and to punish and deter the states that actively sponsor them. But unlike all previous wars, we are using force in pursuit of individuals whom we can only identify as the enemy once we have subjected them to the mechanisms of the criminal justice system—once we have demonstrated that they have engaged in the planning, preparation, or execution of either specific acts of terrorism or a general campaign of terrorism. We have no quarrel with ordinary Afghans or Saudis or Egyptians.

That means that we have to get it right. If the suspects tried, convicted, and sentenced before military tribunals are in fact terrorists, we will have significantly reduced a threat to our national security. If they are not, if they are wrongly convicted due to cases of mistaken identity, or an inability to challenge key evidence, or the difficulty of refuting circumstantial evidence that would normally not be admissible in U.S. courts, or simply through the over zealousness of two out of three military-tribunal judges not subject to ordinary appellate review, we will have sown dragon's teeth. We will be, and will be seen to be, fighting and killing innocent Muslims.

The Ultimate Abuse of Power

The point of the guarantees embedded in the Constitution is precisely to prevent the conviction of innocent people, the ultimate abuse of state power. Those guarantees will protect any U.S. citizens suspected of aiding and abetting terrorism. The guarantees of the German and the Spanish constitutions will protect the suspected terrorists found and tried in those countries (and Spain has said it will not extradite accused terrorists to the United States if they are going to be judged by military tribunals). But in Pakistan, Afghanistan, and even here in the United States in trials of noncitizens, we are proposing to depart fundamentally from those safeguards.

We are fighting and must win a new kind of war. We will ultimately have to craft new rules to govern this type of conflict, both domestically and internationally. But the best way to develop such rules is to work together with our allies and nations across the world that are similarly threatened. We should draw on the experience of nations with long histories of fighting terrorism—Britain, Spain, India, Sri Lanka, South Africa, Colombia, the Philippines. We should devise a system that draws on both national courts and an international tribunal. Setting ourselves up unilaterally as judge, jury, and executioner in closed military tribunals is a recipe for defeat.

7

VIEWPOINT

"Black and brown youths receive harsher treatment than white youths at every stage of the juvenile justice system."

The Juvenile Justice System Discriminates Against Minorities

William Raspberry

In the following viewpoint, syndicated columnist William Raspberry discusses a study that documents racism against blacks and Latinos in the juvenile justice system. According to the study, minority youth are more likely to be arrested, tried, convicted, and incarcerated than white youth. Raspberry asserts that the different treatment may be based in part on how society views young male offenders: White teens are often considered to be "troubled youth" who need help while black teens are seen as thugs who should be thrown in jail.

As you read, consider the following questions:

1. What is the average jail time for whites as opposed to blacks and Hispanics, as cited by the author?
2. According to Raspberry, how much more likely is it that blacks will be sent to prison than whites?
3. In Raspberry's opinion, what would make some of the disparity between black and white offenders disappear?

William Raspberry, ". . . In a Troubled System," *The Washington Post*, April 28, 2000, p. A31.

Maybe today—just days after a 16-year-old black kid allegedly shot up a crowd at the National Zoo in Washington, D.C.—is the wrong time to talk about a new report on the startling racial disparities in the treatment of juvenile offenders.

Then again, maybe it's the perfect time. For our reactions to the suspected zoo shooter—from the initial public reaction to final disposition—are likely to shed light on the reasons behind the disparate treatment.

You know about the Easter Monday 2000 shooting. An 11-year-old boy remains in critical condition after being shot in the head, and six other youngsters are nursing wounds suffered when, following some sort of teenage tiff, the 16-year-old allegedly fired from across Connecticut Avenue into a crowd leaving the zoo.

A Damning Thesis

What you may have missed is the report of a group called Building Blocks for Youth—"And Justice for Some." The report documents as convincingly as I've seen this damning thesis: Black and brown youths receive harsher treatment than white youths at every stage of the juvenile justice system.

The minority youngsters are more likely to be arrested; when arrested, more likely to be jailed or sent to court; when tried, more likely to be convicted; and when convicted, more likely to be given longer prison terms.

Look at some of the specifics: For youths charged with violent offenses, the average jail time is 193 days for whites, 254 for blacks, and 305 for Hispanics. Among those not previously incarcerated, blacks are 6.3 times as likely as whites to be sent to prison—nine times more likely if charged with a violent offense. In the case of drug offenses, blacks are 48 times more likely than whites to be sentenced to juvenile prison.

You could call it rank racism, but that's too easy. It isn't that officials at the various option points between arrest and disposition say the kid is black, so I'll do X, or he's white, so I'll only do Y. The greater likelihood is that they, like the rest of us, respond to the pictures in our heads.

Mention Littleton, Colorado, or Jonesboro, Arkansas [where white teen boys shot classmates at their school], and the picture is likely to be of "troubled" teenagers—perhaps from families that give them too little attention, from schools where they are put down as nerds or geeks, or from other circumstances that "explain" their aberrational behavior.

Mention a shooting in South Central or Hough or Southeast Washington, and the picture is likely to be of an armed thug—bristling for trouble and richly deserving of the full weight of the law.

Length of Imprisonment for Youth Charged with Violent Offenses

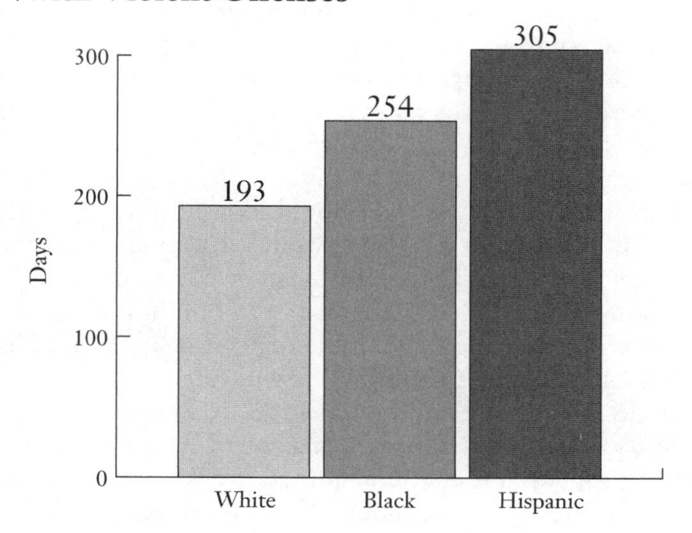

Eileen Poe-Yamagata and Michael A. Jones, "And Justice for Some," www.buildingblocksforyouth.org, April 2000.

In the one case, the questions are about what went wrong; in the other, they are about how best to protect ourselves. The distinction is more vivid yet in the case of nonviolent offenses. Whether you're a cop, a judge or a member of the public, your impulse is to get help for a troubled kid and to throw a thug in jail. I don't doubt that such notions account for some measure of the disparities reported by Building Blocks for Youth. Nor do I doubt that at least some of the disparity would disappear if family income and influence were held constant.

The kid whose family has a little clout and can afford an experienced lawyer may get off with a suspended sentence or a reduced charge for, say, a marijuana offense, while the family without resources is hitting up relatives to raise bail money.

An Unfair System

The point of the Building Blocks report (written by Eileen Poe-Yamagata and Michael Jones of the National Council on Crime and Delinquency and funded by the U.S. Justice Department and several leading foundations) is the manifest unfairness of the system.

But unfairness has different meanings. Clearly it means that two youngsters arrested by the same cop for the same offense ought to be treated similarly through final disposition. But does it also mean that a cop (or a judge or a social worker) is not supposed to factor in his best judgment about what treatment is more appropriate?

Does it mean that a judge should look not merely at the defendant before him but also at what has happened to other members of the offender's race in other courts in other jurisdictions? Given the case made by the Building Blocks report, does fairness dictate more leniency for black and Hispanic kids, or tougher handling for whites?

And in the case of Antoine Jones, the 16-year-old charged as the zoo shooter, what are the black mayor and black chief of police supposed to recommend to a black judge in the interest of justice to the residents of this predominantly black city?

I suspect the answer will depend on whether we come to see him as a troubled and appropriately remorseful youth or as another thug in a city with too many thugs walking around.

VIEWPOINT

> *"When black and white criminals are carefully compared for offense and criminal record, the justice system treats them pretty much the same."*

The Juvenile Justice System Does Not Discriminate Against Minorities

Jared Taylor

Jared Taylor argues in the following viewpoint that a study that purports to show that black youth offenders are six times more likely to be incarcerated than white youth offenders makes no such claim. He contends that the report used misleading language to state this conclusion which is not borne out by evidence, and most of the media accepted the claim as true without checking facts. Assertions of incarceration disparities are nothing more than media hype, he maintains. Taylor, president of the New Century Foundation, a think tank in Washington, D.C., writes frequently on crime.

As you read, consider the following questions:

1. What does the report actually say about black youth and incarceration, according to Taylor?
2. In Taylor's opinion, why are blacks more likely to be imprisoned than whites?
3. Who was misled by the wording in the report, according to the author?

Jared Taylor, "Press Bias on Police Bias," *The Washington Times*, May 29, 2000, p. A19.

"A black youth is six times more likely to be locked up than a white peer, even when charged with a similar crime and when neither has a record. . . ." So began an Associated Press news story picked up uncritically by dozens of papers including *The Washington Post* that helped feed a wave of national breast-beating over the unfairness of the juvenile justice system. The story was about a report put out by a San Francisco organization called Building Blocks for Youth, which claimed to "document the cumulative disadvantage of minority youth" in the face of a biased system.

What the Report Really Says

But is the system really that bad? Are black first-time offenders really six times more likely to go to jail than white first-timers charged with the same crimes? Of course not. To its credit, the Building Blocks for Youth report didn't actually say that. To its great discredit the organization has done nothing to dispel an error that perfectly suits its image of prejudiced law-enforcement. The "six times" figure is probably well on its way into the folklore of racial oppression.

What the report says is that during 1993, black juveniles in several states were six times more likely than whites to get locked up in some kind of public facility. It says nothing about what accounts for this six-fold disparity. This finding is vastly different from the claim that made headlines, namely, that blacks are six times more likely than whites to go to jail when they commit the same crimes and have similar records. The mere fact that more blacks than whites are locked up is something criminologists have known for years and does not necessarily suggest justice system bias at all. It may reflect only higher crime rates among blacks.

The media mischief began when this bit of data was bulleted as a "major finding" at the beginning of the report: "When White youth and minority youth were charged with the same offenses, African-American youth with no prior admissions were six times more likely to be incarcerated in public facilities than White youth with the same background." It sure sounds like a stacked deck in court.

"Perhaps the wording in the bullet was misleading," concedes Eileen Poe-Yamagata, one of the report's co-authors.

> **The Criminal Justice System Is Fair**
>
> Studies show that, with occasional exceptions, virtually everyone gets treated fairly by our criminal justice system. In fact if anything, a black felony defendant is more likely to be acquitted in a jury trial than his white counterpart. It's a myth that our modern legal system is rotten with discrimination. Increased black police officers and judges, for example, haven't reduced the racial disparities in our prisons.
>
> Morgan O. Reynolds, "Racial Profiling Less About Race than You Think," www.ncpa.org, April 9, 2001.

It sure was. It misled nearly every journalist in the country. The *Boston Herald* wrote that "black first-time offenders are six times more likely to be sentenced to prison by juvenile courts than whites." The *Saint Louis Post-Dispatch* led its story with the same shocking finding. The *Chicago Tribune, Cincinnati Enquirer, Cleveland Plain-Dealer* and *Seattle Post-Intelligencer* and plenty of other papers trumpeted the news. William Raspberry agonized over judicial bias in his column. The *Philadelphia Inquirer* wrung its hands over the six times problem in an editorial. It was a startling, incendiary finding and most of the press swallowed it without a gurgle. The *Washington Times* was one of only a handful of newspapers that did not join the pack, baying about racism.

No Racial Bias

If there really were such strong evidence of racial bias in the justice system it would be newsworthy all right, but that is not what the report found because it is not there to be found. Many studies over the years have determined that when black and white criminals are carefully compared for offense and criminal record, the justice system treats them pretty much the same. As for high rates of incarceration for blacks, compelling evidence from the U.S. government's National Crime Victimization Survey suggests that blacks—juvenile and adult—are overrepresented in jails because they commit more crimes, not because of judicial bias.

What are the chances Building Blocks for Youth will issue a correction? "We're not really sure at this point," says Miss Poe-Yamagata. "I had noticed in a few of the articles that there could be a need for that, but there hasn't been an official decision on that." Don't count on one anytime soon. Groups like this thrive on charges of racism, not on sober reporting. It is not likely to be much bothered if a disparity in lock-up rates that probably reflects nothing more than high crime rates among blacks has now been twisted into proof that the system is racist.

Periodical Bibliography

The following articles have been selected to supplement the diverse views presented in this chapter.

America	"The Innocence Protection Act," September 23, 2002.
George P. Fletcher	"War and the Constitution," *American Prospect*, January 1–14, 2002.
George P. Fletcher, Cass R. Sunstein, and Laurence Tribe	"The Military Tribunal Debate," *American Prospect*, February 11, 2002.
John Gibeaut	"Indictment of a System," *ABA Journal*, January 2001.
David Gilbert	"Capitalism and Crisis: Creating a Jailhouse Nation," *Monthly Review*, March 2001.
William Glaberson	"Juries, Their Power Under Siege, Find Their Role Is Being Eroded," *New York Times*, March 2, 2001.
Steven Hawkins	"Lynching Past and Present: Race and the Death Penalty," *New Crisis*, May 2001.
Hank Kalet	"A Penalty for All of Us," *Progressive Populist*, July 15, 2001.
Wendy Kaminer	"Criminally Unjust," *American Prospect*, August 27, 2001.
Heather MacDonald	"The Myth of Racial Profiling," *City Journal*, Spring 2001.
Roger Mahoney	"Defend Life by Taking Life?" *Sojourners*, September/October 2000.
Robert Perske	"Wages of Sin," *Christian Social Action*, February 2002.
William C. Placher and Phyllis Kersten	"'You Were in Prison,'" *Christian Century*, September 26, 2001.
Sheldon Richman	"Military Tribunal Rules Violate the Rule of Law," *Ideas on Liberty*, April 2002.
Jerome H. Skolnick	"The Color of Law," *American Prospect*, July/August 1998.
Anne-Marie Slaughter	"Al Qaeda Should Be Tried Before the World," *New York Times*, November 17, 2001.
Deborah Small	"The War on Drugs Is a War on Racial Justice," *Social Research*, October 2001.
Abraham D. Sofaer and Paul R. Williams	"Doing Justice During Wartime," *Policy Review*, February 2001.
Stuart Taylor Jr.	"Does the Death Penalty Save Innocent Lives?" *National Journal*, May 26, 2001.

CHAPTER 2

Is the Prison System Effective?

Chapter Preface

The Bureau of Justice Statistics (BJS) reports that in 2001, 2.1 million Americans were incarcerated by federal, state, or local authorities, and an additional 4.5 million were on probation or parole. According to the BJS, the U.S. prison population grew an average of 3.6 percent per year between 1995 and 2001. In order to house all those new inmates, federal and state governments built more prisons and the United States experienced a prison boom during the 1990s.

According to some criminal justice experts, prisons are failing in their mission to rehabilitate inmates in preparation for their release back into society. Small-time drug offenders are sentenced to prison instead of receiving treatment for their addiction; thus it is no surprise, these experts maintain, that when the small-timers are released, they go back to drugs and crime to support their habit.

Proponents of "get tough on crime" laws contend, however, that prisons have become a country club for inmates. Convicts eat three meals a day, watch television, read books, play sports, and lift weights, among other activities, all courtesy of American taxpayers. These experts argue that if prisons were actually harsh, punishing places, released inmates would be in no hurry to return and would therefore change their behavior to ensure they stayed out.

Central to the debate over the criminal justice system is whether the role of prisons is to punish or to rehabilitate inmates. The authors in the following chapter examine this issue and others as they debate whether the prison system is an effective solution to crime.

1

VIEWPOINT

"Crime is falling because prisons are filling."

Prisons Are Responsible for the Drop in Crime Rates

Morgan O. Reynolds

In the following viewpoint, Morgan O. Reynolds argues that the crime rate has declined because of new get-tough policies that are putting more criminals in prison. Criminals are aware of the increased likelihood that punishment awaits them, he asserts, and therefore they are making a rational choice to not commit crimes. Studies have found that criminals are more influenced by the certainty of punishment than the severity of punishment. Since the risk of imprisonment has increased, Reynolds maintains, the crime rate has steadily declined. Reynolds is a senior fellow and director of the National Center for Policy Analysis.

As you read, consider the following questions:

1. What evidence does Reynolds present to support his contention that criminals respond to negative incentives?
2. According to Steven Levitt's calculations, how many crimes are eliminated on average for each prisoner locked up?
3. According to a National Association of Science panel, how much violent crime would be prevented by a 50 percent increase in the probability of incarceration as opposed to a 50 percent increase in the length of the imprisonment?

Morgan O. Reynolds, "Does Punishment Deter?" *NCPA Policy Backgrounder*, August 17, 1998.

The nationwide plunge in crime continues to astound scholars and journalists. "This is a humbling time for all crime analysts," says John J. DiIulio, celebrated criminologist and professor at Princeton University.

The FBI's crime index has declined for six straight years, as Figure 1 shows. Every category of crime is lower than in 1991. The murder rate is only two-thirds of the 1991 rate, and violent crime declined 20 percent nationally between 1993 and 1997. Murders and robberies each dropped 9 percent last year alone. Overall, last year's 5 percent decline in violent crime represents a one-year benefit of $20 billion, based on the Department of Justice's estimate that the annual national cost of violent crime (plus drunk driving and arson) is $426 billion.

Punishment for Crime

What explains the sudden decline in crime after a long rise? Better economic conditions? Cultural changes? A more convincing explanation is at hand: Courts have been handing out tougher punishment for crime, and potential criminals know and fear it.

Time was—and not so long ago—when many American courts endorsed the sociological proposition that democratic societies should stress rehabilitation of the offender. Punishment for punishment's sake was deemed a cruel and outmoded approach to crime prevention.

Even today some Americans fail to see the connection between new get-tough policies and recent improvements in the crime rate. "Crime keeps on falling, but prisons keep on filling," a *New York Times* headline declared. The headline writer's attempt at paradox is unwarranted. Crime is falling because prisons are filling.

The new get-tough attitude has brought about significant policy changes.

- More lawbreakers (1.8 million) are behind bars today than ever before.
- New laws have lengthened sentences and imposed tougher restrictions on parole.

The lawbreaker of the 1990s cannot expect the comparatively gentle treatment the courts would have meted out a few years ago. Today, seeing that the law means business, many potential criminals decide to keep out of the law's way. In other words, they decide *not* to rape, steal, rob or kill.

That punishment deters crime is common sense. Observations of human behavior, the opinions of criminals themselves, simple facts about crime and punishment and sophisticated statistical studies all indicate that what matters most to prospective criminals is the certainty and severity of punishment. In other words, negative incentives matter in the business of crime.

This is not to diminish the fundamental and continuing importance of internal restraints: character, morality, virtuous habits. Though hardly a perfect substitute for these brakes on criminal behavior, punishment meted out by the justice system remains a vital complement to minimal morality. For years the U.S. criminal justice system lacked the will or the teeth to punish, especially in dealing with juveniles. But in the past few years deterrence has reasserted itself and has driven crime down.

Crime as a Rational Act

Evidence abounds that law-abiding citizens respond to incentives. Why would criminals be different? We know that criminals avoid knowingly committing crimes in front of the police, which explains why the police interrupt so few crimes in progress. We also know that prison and jail officials manage 1.8 million inmates daily, some of them bad or vicious, with almost no incidents. How do they maintain such order? Through disciplinary measures that inmates heed and respect.

The reality is that the threat of bad consequences, including retribution posed by the legal system, protects life and property against predation. If men were angels, as James Madison said, we'd have no need of government.

Interviews with Criminals

Human action, including criminality, is purposeful behavior. The testimony of criminals provides our strongest evidence that, in the vast majority of cases, lawbreakers are rational. They reason and act like other human beings. Perhaps the best study on this issue among the relatively few available is by criminologists Richard Wright and Scott Decker, who during 1989–90 interviewed 105 active, nonincarcerated residential burglars in St. Louis, Mo.

For example, burglar "Charlie" remarked, "I can go back to selling drugs, [for] which I could lose my ass. If I get caught on burglary, I know I'm guaranteed four years [imprisonment]. I get caught with drugs, I'm a do 30 [years]. So see, I got away from drugs and fell with the number one [offense, burglary]."

Figure 1: 1997 Crime Rates as a Percentage of 1991 Rates

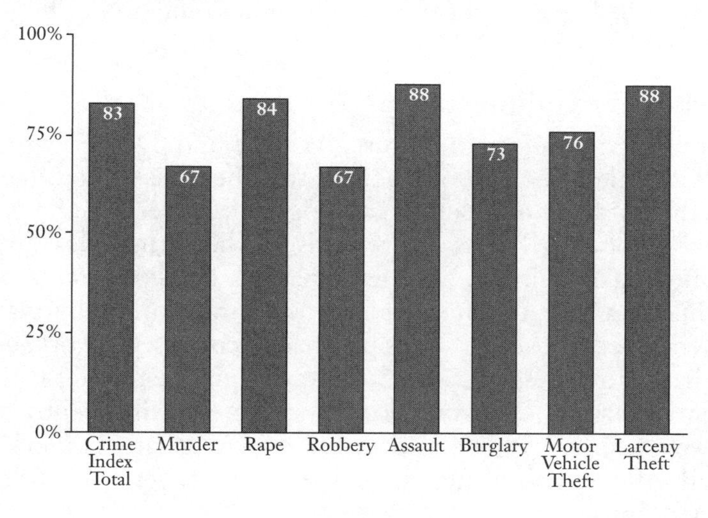

FBI

Other offenders regard robbery, especially armed robbery, as too risky. Burglar No. 013 said, "After my eight years for robbery, I told myself then I'll never do another robbery because I was locked up with so many guys that was doin' 25 to 30 years for robbery and I think that's what made me stick to burglaries, because I had learned that a crime committed with a weapon will get you a lot of time."

Prospective criminals also choose their targets by considering both risk and rewards. For example:

- Burglars avoid neighborhoods that are heavily patrolled

or aggressively policed: "You got to stay away from where the police ride real tough."

- Nine out of 10 burglars say they *always* avoid breaking into an occupied residence: "I rather for the police to catch me vs. a person catching me breaking in their house because the person will kill you. Sometimes the police will tell you, 'You lucky we came before they did.'"

In addition, most burglars have to consciously suppress the fear of capture or work with an accomplice to bolster their confidence. And realistically enough, offenders perceive the chance of being apprehended for a given break-in as extremely slim, partly because they efficiently search the master bedroom first (cash, jewelry, guns) and do not linger inside the target.

Scholarly Opinion

In the criminology literature, Wright and Decker write, "Rational choice theorists believe that the decision to offend is the outcome of a deliberate weighing, however rudimentary, of potential costs and rewards." While criminals sometimes make "hurried, almost haphazard, decisions to offend while in a state of emotional turmoil," most of the burglars mentioned above, for example, had a consistent, workable scheme for assessing risk-and-reward signals emitted by potential targets, knew numerous ways to gain illicit entry to dwellings, had a general plan for searching targets quickly and efficiently and understood how to convert the stolen goods into cash.

Brian Forst, an American University criminologist, wrote, "While the theory of general deterrence has received empirical support for many categories of offenses, such support in crimes of passion and in violent crimes committed by juveniles has been notably absent." Is he wrong? Do murder and rape fit the model? Yes, because even people in a state of rage *choose* when, where and how often to yield to their emotions and impulses. At a minimum, murderers and rapists indulge in more criminal acts at lower anticipated cost (risk of apprehension and punishment). Stanton Samenow, a well-known clinical psychologist and interviewer of thousands of criminals, insists, "The criminal is rational, calculating and deliberate in his actions. Criminals know right from wrong. . . . A habit is not a compulsion. On any occasion, the thief can refrain from stealing if he is in danger of getting caught."

The Impact of Punishment

Only after World War II did scholars begin to study the effects of deterrence. Today a large body of scholarly literature generally confirms the value of punishment in the prevention of crime. Students of the question have come at it from different angles. Some simply ask if punishment deters. Others want to know which deterrent is more effective—certainty of punishment or severity of punishment.

General Evidence That Punishment Deters

Isaac Erhlich's 1973 study of punishment and deterrence is perhaps the most widely cited in the field. Using state data for 1940, 1950 and 1960, Ehrlich found that crime varied inversely with the probability of prison and the average time served.

For each 10 percent rise in a state's prison population, University of Chicago economist Steven Levitt estimated, robberies fall 7 percent, assault and burglary shrink 4 percent each, auto theft and larceny decline 3 percent each, rape falls 2½ percent and murder drops 1½ percent. On average, about 15 crimes are eliminated for each additional prisoner locked up, saving social costs estimated at $53,900—well in excess of the $30,000 it costs annually to incarcerate a prisoner. Another study, by Llad Phillips, found that each year of prison prevented 187 crimes per year.

Certainty of Punishment vs. Severity of Punishment

Scholars regularly consider which provides the greater deterrent. One provocative study involved prisoners and college students. When tested, both groups responded in virtually identical terms. Prisoners could identify their financial self-interest in an experimental setting as well as students could. However, in their decision making, prisoners are much more sensitive to changes in certainty than in severity of punishment. In terms of real-world application, the authors of the study speculate that "long prison terms are likely to be more impressive to lawmakers than lawbreakers."

Supporting evidence for this viewpoint comes from a National Academy of Sciences panel which estimated that a 50 percent increase in the probability of incarceration prevents about twice as much violent crime as a 50 percent increase in the average term of incarceration.

Figure 2: Crime and Punishment, Selected Years, 1950–1996

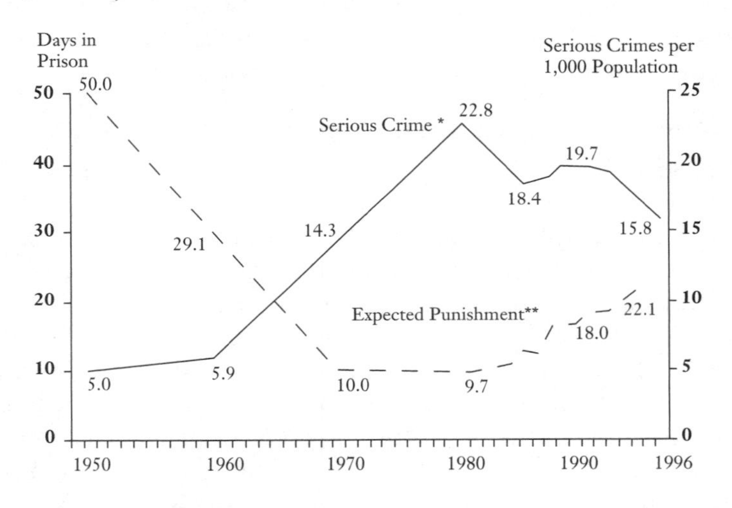

* Defined as FBI Index crimes of violence (murder and non-negligent manslaughter, forcible rape, robbery, aggravated assault) plus burglary, per thousand population.

** Defined as probability of prison per serious Index crime × median days served in prison per serious Index crime.

Morgan O. Reynolds, "Crime and Punishment in America: 1997 Update," National Center for Policy Analysis, NCPA Report No. 209, September 1997.

Likelihood of punishment often tends to affect property crimes more than violent and sexual offenses. This point is borne out in a study by Itzhak Goldberg and Frederick Nold showing that in communities where more people report burglaries to the police, fewer burglaries take place. A tendency to report crimes has an aggregate deterrent effect on criminals because it raises expectations of punishment.

Nonetheless, severity of punishment remains crucial for deterrence. "A prompt and certain slap on the wrist," criminologist Ernest van den Haag wrote, "helps little." Or, as Milwaukee Judge Ralph Adam Fine wrote, "We keep our hands out of a flame because it hurt the very first time (not the second, fifth or 10th time) we touched the fire."

To a degree, the certainty vs. severity argument is academic. As Donald Lewis wrote in 1986 after surveying the economic literature on crime, "The bulk of evidence resulting from the competent use of theory and statistics supported the existence of a deterrent effect of both imprisonment risk and longer sentences." Lewis emphasized that a substantial body of evidence is consistent with "the existence of a deterrent effect from longer sentences." V.K. Mathur reached similar conclusions after studying 1960 and 1970 data for U.S. cities of over 100,000 population.

If Punishment Deters, Why Are So Many People in Prison?

If the United States, with so many people in prison, has one of the world's highest crime rates, does this imply that prison does not work? Scholar Charles Murray has examined this question and concluded that the answer is no. Instead, the nation has had to imprison more people in recent years because it failed to do so earlier. Murray compared the record of the risk of imprisonment in England to that in the United States.

- In England the risk of going to prison for committing a crime fell by about 80 percent over a period of 40 years—and the English crime rate rose gradually.
- By contrast, the risk of going to prison in the U.S. fell by 64 percent in just 10 years starting in 1961—and the U.S. crime rate shot up.

In the United States, it was not a matter of crime's increasing so fast that the rate of imprisonment could not keep up. Rather, the rate of imprisonment began to fall first. By the time the U.S. began incarcerating more criminals in the mid-1970s, huge increases were required to bring the risk of imprisonment up to the crime rate. It is more difficult to reestablish a high rate of imprisonment after the crime rate has escalated than to maintain a high risk of imprisonment from the outset, Murray concluded.

However, the American experience showed that it is possible for imprisonment to stop a rising crime rate and then gradually begin to push it down. The American crime rate peaked in 1980, a few years after the risk of imprisonment reached its nadir. Since then, as the risk of imprisonment has increased, with few exceptions the rates of serious crimes have retreated in fits and starts to levels of 20 or more years ago.

2

VIEWPOINT

"While imprisonment may have some impact on crime . . . it is hardly the only social policy option that may influence crime rates."

Factors Other than Prison May Be Responsible for the Drop in Crime Rates

Marc Mauer

Marc Mauer argues in the following viewpoint that while incarceration *may* have an impact on crime rates, other factors play a role as well. He examines crime and incarceration rates during a twenty-five year period and finds that while the incarceration rate steadily climbed, the crime rate fluctuated. The most significant change in crime rate during this period was for burglary, which fell 41 percent. However, Mauer maintains that prisons did not see a surge in the number of burglars who were sent to prison. Therefore, Mauer concludes, the data does not conclusively link imprisonment rates with crime rates. Mauer, the assistant director of The Sentencing Project, a national organization that promotes reform in the criminal justice and prison systems, is the author of *Race to Incarcerate*, from which this viewpoint is excerpted.

As you read, consider the following questions:

1. How did the murder rate in 1995 compare to the murder rate in 1970, as cited by the author?
2. Why are the differing trends in juvenile and adult violence significant, in Mauer's opinion?

The quarter-century-long prison buildup that resulted in a sextupling of the prison population is unprecedented in American history, and perhaps that of any modern nation using this institution as a means of crime control. The costs of this buildup, both in fiscal and human terms, have been substantial, with corrections spending now approaching $40 billion a year nationally.

Prison and Crime Rate

Much discussion, not to mention hyperbole, has taken place in recent years regarding the effect of the prison population increase on the crime rate. To the extent that incarceration is viewed as a natural response to crime, this would appear to be a reasonable relationship to examine. Before assessing this relationship, though, consider for a moment the larger context in which the question is posed. Locking up a convicted offender may indeed have some impact on crime. The fact that Charles Manson spends his years in a prison cell no doubt has reduced the number of additional persons he might have victimized. But most inmates are not of the Manson variety. Over half of all state and federal prison inmates are currently serving time for a non-violent drug or property offense. While many of these offenders have had prior criminal convictions, the policy decision regarding their sentencing involves a consideration of whether spending $20,000 a year to incarcerate them is the wisest course of action. The alternative is not to do nothing but, rather, to explore whether some combination of community supervision, victim restitution, required treatment, and other conditions would more effectively respond to the needs of both victim and offender.

While imprisonment may have some impact on crime, either by incapacitating offenders for a period of time or by deterring inmates or potential offenders, it is hardly the only social policy option that may influence crime rates. What might other measures look like? High school graduation rates have been inching upwards in recent years. Might this have an impact on crime, either by making young graduates more employable or increasing their self-esteem? Divorce in the United States is far more common than a generation ago, as are single-parent families. How do these factors affect crime rates? How does this compare with the experience in other nations? What has been the impact of raising the minimum wage, or the advent of NAFTA, or community policing, or a variety of other social and economic changes?

Some of these factors have been examined in detail by researchers, while others have received less attention. The point is that they illustrate the complexity of understanding why crime rates might rise or fall over a period of time. Our exploration of the relationship between incarceration and crime needs to be understood in this larger context.

The Bigger Picture

From the vantage point of the late 1990s, one might conclude, as have many political leaders, that prison is "working." After all, both overall crime rates and violent crime rates began a steady decline in 1992, coinciding with a period in which the prison population was steadily rising—ergo, there must be some relationship. However, if we examine a broader time period, beginning just prior to the prison buildup that began in the 1970s, the picture gets cloudy. As we can see for the 25-year period displayed in Figure 1, there

Figure 1. Incarceration and Crime Rates, 1970–1995

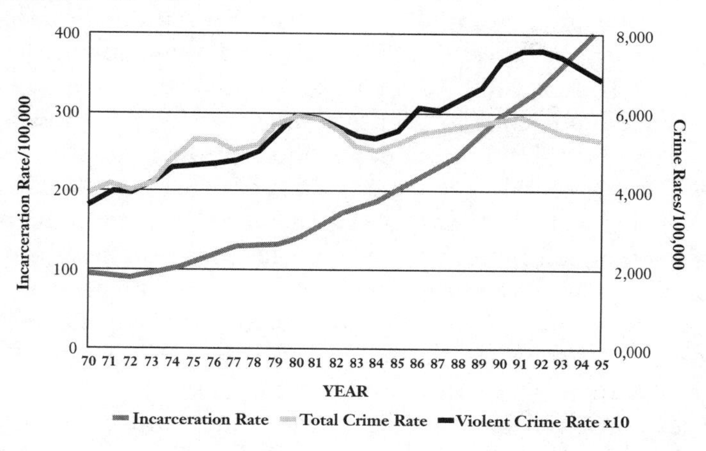

Bureau of Justice Statistics, *Sourcebook of Criminal Justice Statistics*, 1996.

are essentially four distinct periods of rise and fall in crime rates. (In the figure, violent crime rates are multiplied by a factor of ten so that trends can be discerned on this scale.) Overall crime rates generally rose in the 1970s, then declined from 1980 to 1984, increased again from 1984 to 1991, and then declined through 1995. With only minor exceptions, violent crime rates have followed this pattern as well. Each of these phases, of course, occurred during a time when the prison population was continuously rising. Thus, a steadily increasing prison population has twice coincided with periods of increase in crime and twice with declines in crime.

The fact that the relationships are inconsistent does not mean that rising imprisonment had *no* impact on crime, but neither does it lend itself to a statement that incarceration had an unambiguously positive impact in this area. What is critical to note here as well is the scope of the changes being discussed—the unprecedented 328 percent increase in the rate of incarceration from 1970 to 1995. Property crime rates finally reached a 20-year low in 1995, but were still higher than in 1970 before the prison buildup began; and violent crime, with the exception of murder, was still consistently higher than the 1970 rate.

The Murder Rate

The decline in murder is not inconsequential, of course, and deserves close scrutiny. By 1995, national murder rates had declined by 20 percent to 8.2 per 100,000 population from a peak of 10.2 per 100,000 in 1980, a significant decline (and continued to decline to 6.8 per 100,000 in 1997). Yet looking again at the 1970–95 period, we find that the murder rate in 1995 was essentially the same as the rate of 8.3 per 100,000 in 1970. Thus, the best that can be said about changes in homicide is that these rates were *no worse* in 1995 than in 1970 despite the addition of nearly one million prison inmates.

Further, one's risk of being murdered is very dependent on one's place of residence. In general, U.S. cities became less safe during this 25-year period. Sixteen of the 20 largest U.S. cities registered increases in murder rates during this time, with ten of these displaying a rise of 50 percent or more.

Overall, the murder rate has declined, and that is a welcome development. Whether much or most of this decline is attributable to increased incarceration, though, is not at all clear.

A critical issue in this regard concerns differing trends in homicide rates among juveniles and adults. From 1984 to 1993, for example, homicide rates among white males in the 14–17 age group doubled from 6.9 per 100,000 to 14.4 per 100,000, while for black males, the rate more than quadrupled, increasing from 33.4 to 151.6 per 100,000. For males 25 and over, though, homicide rates for both blacks and whites declined by more than 20 percent. Overall, 14–17-year-old males constituted 6.3 percent of homicide offenders in the mid-1980s; this proportion doubled to 13 percent by the early 1990s. By the mid-1990s, though, the juvenile murder rates began to drop precipitously. Between 1994 and 1995, juvenile homicides dropped 17 percent, with the bulk of this decline occurring among black males.

The differing trends in juvenile and adult violence are significant because juveniles are essentially unaffected by the dramatic growth of the adult prison population. While more adult offenders were incapacitated in prison during this period, and therefore unable to commit crimes while locked up, this did not generally apply to juveniles. Therefore, whatever combination of circumstances contributed first to the rise and then to the decline of the juvenile homicide rate, the prison buildup was not one of these factors.

Other Factors

Other factors that may influence trends in this area include what has been described as an "attrition of the at-risk population." This refers to the fact that the low-income minorities who are disproportionately murder victims and offenders have suffered high death rates in recent years from a variety of factors—violence, AIDS, accidents, and various preventable illnesses. In comparison to the homicide rate for black men aged 15–24 that reached 167 per 100,000 in 1993, for example, deaths for black males ages 25–34 from HIV infection reached 117 per 100,000. A study of young black men in Philadelphia over the years 1987–90 found that 40 percent had had at least one emergency room visit for a serious violent assault.

Looking at violent crime overall, a number of studies have attempted to quantify the impact that rising imprisonment has had on these rates. The National Research Council of the National Academy of Sciences has estimated the impact of imprisonment on violent crime rates and concluded that the tripling of time served per violent crime from 1975 to 1989 had "very little" impact; it recommended that "*preventive* strategies may be as important as criminal justice *responses* to violence." Similar findings have been seen in other nations. In a report for the Home Office in the United Kingdom, analysts concluded that a 25 percent rise in the prison population would result in a 1 percent decline in overall crime rates.

The Burglary Rate

Other U.S. studies have tended to show that, to the extent that prison has any impact on crime, it is more likely to be observed in rates of property crime. An assessment of the incapacitating impact of the addition of more than 100,000 offenders to California's prisons and jails during the decade of the 1980s, for example, concluded that the bulk of the crime that may have been prevented through incarceration was concentrated in burglary—although even here the results were expressed with caution. Since most of the burglary decline was among juveniles, whereas the incarceration increase primarily affected adults, it is not clear how direct this relationship may have been.

At the national level, the most significant area of change in crime rates for the period 1980–95 has also been in the area of burglary. As we can see in Table 1, although violent crime rates rose by 15 percent during this period, crime rates overall declined by 11 percent and property crime was down by 14 percent. The decline in burglary was the most substantial by far, falling by 41 percent, and accounting for fully 92 percent of the decline in property crime in this fifteen-year period.

To what extent, then, can we conclusively attribute this decline in burglary to increased incarceration? An examination of changes in the composition of the prison population for the years 1980–95 does not suggest that an increase in

Table 1. Crime Rates and Incarceration, 1980–1995

Crime	Rate per 100,000		% Change	% Change in State Prisoners
	1980	1995	1980–1995	1980–1995
All	5950	5278	–11%	+234%
Violent	597	685	+15%	+168%
Property	5353	4593	–14%	+158%
Burglary	1684	988	–41%	+114%

FBI Uniform Crime Reports 1995; Bureau of Justice Statistics, *Corrections Populations in the United States, 1994 and 1995.*

the number of imprisoned burglars was necessarily the primary factor at work. As Table 1 shows, during this period the overall number of state prison inmates rose by 234 percent, violent offenders by 168 percent, property offenders by 158 percent, and burglars by 114 percent. Thus, we see relatively modest changes in crimes rates for nonburglary offenses despite substantial increases in imprisonment, but a considerable decline in the burglary rate despite a lower rate of increase in the number of incarcerated burglars. This does not suggest that the imprisonment of more burglars had no effect, but it should cause us to look to other factors that may provide a more full interpretation.

Drug Crimes

In looking at other possible explanations, we find that a certain and perhaps substantial portion of the burglaries may have been replaced by other kinds of criminal activity—most notably, drug crimes. The difficulty in quantifying this precisely relates to the way in which crime is measured. When we speak of the "crime rate," official measures refer to the FBI's annual Uniform Crime Reports, a national survey of eight crimes—murder, rape, robbery, aggravated assault, burglary, larceny, auto theft, and arson. These are among the most serious and common of crimes, at least of those which can be measured. "Victimless" crimes, though, cannot be accounted for by any police agency. So, personal drug use or drug sales, or gambling or consensual vice affairs do not result in a victim who reports such crimes to the police.

While there is no means of knowing exactly how many drug crimes were committed during the 1980s, evidence suggests that there may have been significant increases in many cities. Even though casual drug use had been declining since 1979, an increasing proportion of total drug consumption consisted of hard-core drug users, whose numbers had not declined. The irony of these trends is that the decline in casual use, primarily among middle-class users, predated the stepped-up pace of the drug war and was not a result of increased law enforcement efforts. Rather, these declines paralleled declines in other unhealthy lifestyle choices, such as cigarette and alcohol consumption, and can be seen as part of a broader trend toward healthier lifestyles. Hard-core users, though, who were disproportionately low-income, registered no declines in overall use despite being more likely to be subjected to arrest and prosecution.

As crack cocaine made its entry into urban areas beginning in the mid-1980s, new opportunities arose to make money quickly by becoming a street-level seller. While drug arrest rates are not necessarily a direct indicator of drug activity (certainly less so than for offenses such as murder or armed robbery), they nearly doubled from 1980 to 1990, an indicator of a potential increase in these activities.

Burglary Versus Drug-Selling

In looking at the possible displacement of burglary to drug-selling, contrast the two crimes as a means of making money. Burglary involves entering a home illegally, never being certain whether the occupant is home or might even be armed. If small items such as cash or jewelry are not readily apparent, burglary requires stealing bulkier items such as televisions and sound systems, as well as having ready transportation for them. These must then be fenced to be turned into cash at a small fraction of the actual value.

Drug-selling, on the other hand, is much simpler in most respects. All it requires is a willing supplier and a vacant street corner. Transactions are completed in cash with no middleman. Selling drugs is not without its dangers, of course, either from rival drug dealers or the police; but in comparison to burglary it has a number of advantages for the potential offender. At least to a certain extent, the burglar of the 1980s may have become the drug seller of the 1990s.

Beginning in the mid-1980s, burglaries may have also been displaced to robberies as well. While burglary and robbery rates had moved in parallel fashion for about ten years, robbery rates began to increase in 1985 and continued to do so through the early 1990s, while burglary was steadily declining. For a drug addict seeking to obtain money to buy drugs, robbery may prove to be a quicker means of obtaining cash than burglary.

What we see overall in looking at crime rates over the 25-year period of rising incarceration is no dramatic decline, despite the unprecedented increase in the number of prisoners.

3

VIEWPOINT

"Rather than just churning people through the revolving door of the criminal justice system, drug courts use a mix of sanctions and incentives to help these folks to get their acts together so they won't be back."

Drug Courts Reduce Recidivism

Joseph R. Biden

Joseph R. Biden is a senator from Delaware and the chairman of the Senate Judiciary Subcommittee on Crime and Drugs. The following viewpoint is a statement he made at an oversight hearing on drug courts in which he argues that drug courts are a cost-effective way to deal with nonviolent offenders who need drug treatment. He asserts that without treatment, drug offenders will return to a life of crime after leaving prison. However, addicts who undergo treatment, such as that mandated by drug courts, are much more likely to remain drug-free and out of trouble after their release.

As you read, consider the following questions:

1. What percentage of U.S. prisoners are incarcerated because of a drug-related crime, as cited by the author?
2. Why does Biden believe that the 30 percent of the drug court participants who went to jail are another example of the program's success?

Joseph R. Biden, statement to the Jr. Senate Subcommittee on Youth Violence—Oversight Hearing on Drug Courts, October 3, 2000.

I have been involved with drug courts since their inception and I believe in them. And, as the author—along with Senator Arlen Specter—of legislation to reauthorize the drug court program, I look forward to exploring how we can help them work even better. . . . Let me take a minute to thank Judge Richard Gebelein for being here. Not only is Judge Gebelein one of the nation's foremost experts on drug courts, but he also is in charge of the drug court program in my home state of Delaware. I have been an observer in Judge Gebelein's Drug Court—he is known as a "tough judge," but he's also smart enough to know that the old system of locking up every drug offender and throwing away the key—with no treatment and no supervision upon release was failing our criminal justice system and the public at large.

Drug Courts

In the 1994 Crime Law, Congress created a grant program to fund drug courts because we believed that they were a cost-effective, innovative way to deal with non-violent offenders in need of drug treatment.

And since then, drug courts have taken off. There are 533 drug courts currently operating throughout the country, with an additional 293 courts being planned. Drug courts are as much about fighting crime as they are about reducing illegal drugs. It is no secret that there is a strong link between drugs and crime. As one of our witnesses today, Steven Belenko, well knows—because he literally wrote the book on this at National Center on Addiction and Substance Abuse (CASA)—80 percent of those incarcerated today are there because of a crime associated with drug or alcohol abuse or addiction; either they have a history of substance abuse or addiction, they were high when they committed their crime, they violated drug or alcohol laws, or they stole property to buy drugs.

The most recent Arrestee Drug Use Monitoring Program (ADAM) data revealed that more than half of adult male arrestees in the 34 ADAM sites tested positive for drug use at the time of arrest.

Drug courts take non-violent drug-related offenders and closely supervise them as they address the root of their criminal problem. This task is made more difficult by the fact that the root problem is a chronic, relapsing condition—addiction.

Let me let you in on a little secret—if we just lock these folks up and don't treat them, they are going to commit crimes again and again and again. Treatment helps to break that escalating cycle of drug-related criminal behavior.

Impressive Results

To date, nearly 200,000 people have entered drug court programs and the results have been impressive. About 70 percent of the drug court program participants have either stayed in the program or completed it successfully. That is more than twice the retention rate of most traditional treatment programs.

The Judge's Role in Drug Courts

The drug court judge plays the key role in the proceedings and engages directly in conversation with the participant. In addition, although the traditional judge's role in criminal cases is to punish offenders, the drug court judge plays a very untraditional role of also rewarding and praising participants when they do well or achieve specific goals. This combination of sanctions and rewards that typify most drug courts may be another important explanation for their high retention rates.

There is some evidence that drug court participants also view the judge's role as a key component of the drug court. In a 1997 survey of a nonrepresentative sample of drug court participants, 75% said that the fact that a judge monitors their treatment progress was a very important difference between the drug court and prior treatment program experience, 82% cited the possibility of sanctions for noncompliance as a very important difference, and 70% of respondents thought that the opportunity to talk about their progress and problems with a judge was a "very important" factor in keeping them in the program.

Steven Belenko, congressional testimony, April 4, 2000.

The other 30 percent of the participants went to jail. And I think that should be heralded as a success of the drug court program as well. Without drug courts, this 30 percent would have been unsupervised, not monitored, and unless they happened to be unlucky enough to use drugs or commit a crime near a cop, they would still be on the streets abusing drugs and committing crime. Drug courts provide the oversight to make sure that does not happen.

Rather than just churning people through the revolving door of the criminal justice system, drug courts use a mix of sanctions and incentives to help these folks to get their acts together so they won't be back. When they graduate from drug court programs they are clean and sober and more prepared to participate in society.

In order to graduate from most drug courts, participants are required to finish high school or obtain a GED, hold down a job, keep up with financial obligations including drug court fees and child support payments. They are also required to have a sponsor who will keep them on track.

Drug courts work. And that is not just my opinion. Drug courts are effective at taking offenders with little previous treatment history and keeping them in treatment. Treatment experts agree that the longer someone stays in treatment, the more likely that person is to remain drug-free and to become a productive, tax-paying member of society. That may be why drug courts are getting results.

Drug courts reduce recidivism. Though post-program recidivism rates vary between drug courts, consider the impact of the Jefferson County, Kentucky drug court: Thirteen percent of the graduates of that program were reconvicted for a felony, compared to 60 percent of non-graduates and 55 percent of the comparison group.

Drug courts also reduce future drug use. An average of 10 percent of drug court participants have positive drug tests compared to 31 percent of those on probation. And drug courts are cost-effective. According to a study of the Portland, Oregon drug court, for every $1 spent on the drug court, $2.50 is saved in avoided costs such as criminal justice costs, public assistance and medical claims. If you factor in larger costs—such as victimization and theft—there is a savings of $10 for every tax dollar spent on drug courts. Just as important, scarce prison beds are freed up for violent criminals.

Harder to quantify is what I believe may be the most important impact of drug courts. Nearly two-thirds of drug court participants are parents of young children. After getting sober through the coerced treatment mandated by the court, many of these individuals are able to be real parents again. And more than 1,000 drug-free babies have been born to female drug court participants, a sizable victory for society and the budget alike.

New innovative and effective programs like drug courts don't come along often. When they do, we should make sure that we do everything possible to make sure that they continue to succeed.

4

VIEWPOINT

"The drug courts' results, as yet, don't speak for themselves."

Drug Courts Are Counterproductive

Eric Cohen

In the following viewpoint, Eric Cohen maintains that drug courts—programs that emphasize therapy and close supervision for drug offenders—are a "feel-good" alternative to prison that have not yet proven themselves effective in reducing recidivism. Most courts have not been in existence long enough to provide accurate records of long-term success. In addition, Cohen asserts, the program totally ignores such concepts as morality and right versus wrong, concentrating instead on transforming the criminal justice system into a therapeutic justice system whose purpose is to focus on the individual needs of the offender. Cohen is the managing editor of the *Public Interest.*

As you read, consider the following questions:

1. According to the author, what are the judges, lawyers, and counselors involved in drug courts called?
2. What were the three major problems with the available drug court studies, according to the General Accounting Office?
3. What is the most important factor in the apparent success of drug courts, in James Nolan's opinion?

Eric Cohen, "The Drug Court Revolution," *Weekly Standard,* December 27, 1999, pp. 20–23.

At a 1999 Washington, D.C., Drug Court "graduation"—a monthly event for drug defendants who have successfully stayed in treatment—Mark Williams stole the show. Williams, a transvestite dressed in checkered hot pants with matching pocketbook, gave spirited testimony. "I want to thank God. And all my lawyers. And I want to say that you've got to want to stop smoking. You've got to put your mind to it."

Graduation

The rest of the graduating class—about 20 in all—whooped and hollered from the jury box. Judge Russell Canan, who was presiding over the ceremony, couldn't help but chuckle. "This is one of the happier days we have in Drug Court," said Canan. "The people we are honoring here today have gained some respect for the law and for themselves." Williams, by the way, is still awaiting trial on prostitution charges. "He's very creative," his lawyer told me. "Very smart."

After the speech and the applause, the clerk read Williams's case, a misdemeanor drug charge. Then the case was dropped—the reward for the "client" (as all defendants are called) having completed the drug court program, a year-long regimen of therapy and frequent court visits.

In addition to getting his drug charge dropped or reduced, each of the graduates receives a certificate of achievement and a copy of Iyanla Vanzant's 1993 book *Acts of Faith: Daily Meditations for People of Color.* Most of the graduates make speeches—very heartfelt, gracious testimonials. They thank the judge, their treatment counselor, and (some of them, anyway) God. This is, they say, a new beginning.

The event is moving, and perfectly attuned to our therapeutic age. Which is exactly the way the drug court "professionals" (as the lawyers, judges, and counselors who run the nation's drug courts call themselves) have designed it to be. Graduations should be "used to capture the public's interest and garner favorable media publicity," writes Judge Stephen Marcus, one of the gurus of the drug court movement. "The Drug Court graduation is the Super Bowl, NBA Finals, and World Series all rolled into one." The "emotional appeal" and "tears of joy" make journalists, politicians, and lawyers into "immediate converts."

The Cutting Edge

Drug courts are the cutting edge of therapeutic jurisprudence, the latest panacea in the ongoing war against drugs. They are the brainchild of [former] Attorney General Janet Reno, who organized the first drug court in 1989 when she was state's attorney for Dade County, Florida.

Reno's vision—a courtroom unencumbered by traditional rules, a criminal justice system that focuses on the "individual needs of the client" rather than equal justice for all, cooperative therapy rather than adversarial trials—has taken the nation by storm. In 1994 there were only 12 drug courts nationwide. Now in 1999 there are almost 400, with hundreds more in the planning stages, backed by over $100 million in federal seed money. Some 140,000 defendants who would otherwise have been prosecuted for non-violent drug offenses have enrolled in drug courts since 1989.

Perhaps as significant, the drug court advocacy machine is firmly in place—and growing. There is a National Drug Court Institute; a drug court office in the Department of Justice; a drug court journal; hundreds of national, state, and local associations for drug court professionals; and an endless stream of resource guides and pamphlets selling the concept with all the public relations savvy of Madison Avenue—think *Chicken Soup for the Addict.* This elaborate promotional apparatus, it turns out, is all the more necessary, because the drug courts' results, as yet, don't speak for themselves. . . .

No Moral Judgments

Strikingly, in all the hundreds of pages of workbooks, self-assessment guides, and personality tests, there is never a mention of morality, character, virtue, or right and wrong. One personality test asks the clients if they "turn to God" for answers. A yes response means—categorically—that "you are in the late stage of addiction."

When I ask a number of the therapists and the judge whether they try to teach any moral lessons to their "clients," they all look stunned, then offended. "We don't frame it as a moral lesson. Your morality isn't necessarily my morality," says Suzzette Brann, the drug court program director. "We don't try to dictate judgments," says Rashida Mims, assistant treatment coordinator. "We don't do that. We can't do that. If I were to attempt to dictate my values on someone I'd be doing them a disservice." Says Judge Canan: "My personal morals may or may not be meaningful to someone else."

Nevertheless, the drug court program does, at its best, teach some moral lessons—if for no other reason than that clients are required to show up on time, hand in assignments, and examine their lives. More important, offenders must remain drug-free to "graduate." Everyone in the program takes two drug tests a week—one on Monday, one on Thursday. A positive test results in "sanctions"—typically three days of "motivational jail." Many participants are sanctioned a number of times before finally staying clean long enough (three months) to graduate. Such relapses are, according to the therapists, part of the recovery.

Advocates claim that drug courts are a "miracle," a "new reality," "our last, best hope." The statistics they cite seem impressive: According to the Department of Justice's drug court program office and the National Association of Drug Court Professionals, 70 percent of all drug court participants have either finished the program or stayed in treatment; 90 percent of drug tests have been clean; and the recidivism rate for drug court graduates is only 4 percent, compared to "well over 50 percent" of defendants who go through the "traditional adjudication process."

Likewise, the drug court story is heroic, inspirational, a grand social drama with progressive judges and therapists as the protagonists. "A revolution has been going on in the criminal justice system over the past ten years," writes Judge Tauber. "We understood it would take a new kind of community . . . a circle of interveners . . . to restore our cities and our people to health."

A Closer Look

A closer look at the statistics, however, tells a far less heroic tale. The most extensive independent evaluation of the nation's drug courts—conducted by the General Accounting

Office in 1997—concluded that current evidence "did not firmly establish whether drug court programs were successful in reducing drug relapse and offender recidivism." The GAO report cited three major problems with the available studies: Most drug court programs were still in their first or second year of operation; most courts did not keep follow-up data on the rate at which "clients" relapsed or were rearrested; and most studies made no comparison between drug court participants and nonparticipants.

Prison Is Effective

Although some people are not deterred by prison, others are. In fact, those who promote alternatives to prison almost always propose using the threat of imprisonment to make alternative sentences more effective. If the threat of imprisonment does not deter dealers, why bother?

Steve Easton, *USA Today*, September 30, 2002.

Other studies by outside agencies—including the Rand Corporation and the American Bar Association—have found that drug courts have had no discernible effect on crime rates. James Nolan, a sociologist whose recent book *The Therapeutic State* devotes a chapter to drug courts, found that despite the claims of drug court advocates, the most important factor in the apparent success of drug courts is the criminal history of the defendants, not the treatment program. In addition, Nolan found that many of the leading studies are based on questionable, often misleading assumptions—such as excluding early dropouts from the calculation of success rates or counting as success stories individuals who have stayed in the program for more than a year (despite the fact that such career participants have not graduated because they routinely fail their drug tests).

In fact, many drug court professionals reject on principle evaluations of their program according to such empirical, hardheaded criteria as recidivism, relapse rates, and urinalysis testing. They believe, as one put it, that an emphasis on statistics undermines "the real human realities, the changed lives." As Judge Lawrence Terry puts it, we need to "reeducate judges about what success is." A professor of criminal justice at

Florida International University conducted a study that found "little difference between persons remaining in the [drug court] program and those who have not." Still, he concluded that "there is absolutely no question that the drug court is having a very positive effect upon the lives of many people."

The Future of Criminal Justice

No one doubts that the drug court movement will expand, even though its effectiveness remains in serious question. But the rise of therapeutic jurisprudence raises sobering questions about the future of American criminal justice: Is the purpose of courts to "meet the individual needs" of defendants, as the drug court literature routinely assumes? Are justice and therapy one and the same thing? Should judges really play the role of "confessor, cheerleader, and mentor" to the accused who come before them? In the present euphoria over the "drug court revolution," these questions are almost never pondered.

For the fact is that the most passionate advocates for drug courts have a thoroughgoing contempt for "traditional justice." When they call the present system "adversarial" they mean to disparage it, and they mock as antiquated the idea that a judge should be a "dispassionate, disinterested magistrate." They see drug courts as the first step in the transformation of the courts into a wholly therapeutic enterprise. They want to expand the therapeutic model to cases of domestic violence, larceny, prostitution, and even rape. The individuals who commit these crimes are sick, they insist, and should be treated by therapists rather than punished and exiled.

There is no doubt something very pragmatic and sensible about trying to get addicts off drugs, which explains why many prominent conservatives—James Q. Wilson, John J. DiIulio Jr., Jeb Bush, Rudolph Giuliani—have had nice things to say about drug courts. Indeed, when it comes to dealing with most drug-related misdemeanors, drug courts are actually more demanding and coercive than the usual suspended sentence and probation. Offenders who would otherwise be unwatched or at best loosely monitored are instead kept to a rigorous schedule and drug-tested twice a week. Moreover, the best drug courts process cases quickly, which, as Wilson argues, links crime and punishment in the defendant's mind.

What's more, there is no question that the present system—the revolving door of drugs and crime—is in need of reform. As DiIulio wrote, two million prisoners, roughly a quarter of them drug-only offenders, are enough. A self-governing people should not abandon the effort to help drug offenders become decent citizens again. The principles that underlie this effort, however, are important. And it is here that the drug court revolution is most worrisome.

The Washington, D.C., Drug Court tells its clients that lifelong therapy is a "part of healthy living." The evidence so far—from the entrenched moral relativism of the therapists to the transformation of lawyers and judges into "helping professionals"—suggests that therapeutic justice will lead not to the remoralization of society but to the rise of a therapeutic state. Instead of an explosion in the prison population, then, we would have an explosion in the patient population. This is not an outcome that a free society should welcome.

VIEWPOINT

"Research has shown that a person who has advanced their education and received counseling while in prison is much less likely to return to prison than someone who has been idle during their incarceration."

Prisons Should Rehabilitate Inmates

Charles Wampler

Charles Wampler is a prisoner at the Chillicothe Correctional Institute in Ohio. In the following viewpoint, Wampler contends that prisons should rehabilitate inmates by offering mandatory self-improvement classes, education, counseling, and vocational training for prisoners. He argues that requiring self-improvement classes benefits both the prisoner and society because, once released, these prisoners are more likely to find jobs and are less likely to commit crimes and return to prison. Wampler asserts that society and inmates would be better off if inmates served a shorter sentence with required education and counseling goals than a longer sentence with no education or counseling.

As you read, consider the following questions:

1. What are the two main types of crime, according to Wampler?
2. In the author's opinion, what is the problem with the self-improvement programs offered in most prisons?
3. What should a criminal be told upon entering prison, according to Wampler?

It seems that our representatives are mainly concerned with doing what is politically comfortable. It seems as though they feel that the only way to keep public support is to tell the voters what they think the voters want to hear. But, what this country desperately needs is politicians who are not afraid to leave the well-beaten path and have the guts to strike out in new directions to find solutions that actually work instead of looking for answers that sound good. For much too long, the people we have trusted to come up with the answers have continually promised us results through stiffer penalties and longer prison sentences. Over the past several years, we have clearly seen that this answer is totally inadequate.

There are two main types of crime. One is a crime that is committed in the heat of passion, where the perpetrator is thinking of nothing but committing the act. The other is a crime that is planned out and the perpetrator does not believe that he can get caught. How can the possible penalty prevent someone from committing a crime when the person isn't even considering the possibility of getting caught, yet alone what the punishment might be?

Rehabilitation Versus Punishment

It is easy to understand how the focus has changed from rehabilitation to punishment, but basically all we are doing now is keeping a criminal locked up for a little while longer. In the end most of the criminals will still be returned to society and the odds are strong that they will have nothing to show for their time in prison except for an even more bitter outlook on life. So we spend millions of dollars to build more and more prisons to warehouse our criminals and in the end many of those criminals will be released with nothing better to do than return to preying on their community. In essence, we all become victims. We spend millions of dollars to build prisons and millions more to maintain them and care for the inmates confined in them, so that many of these inmates that we support for years can get out and commit another crime and start the entire process over again.

Why do our politicians continually ask us to support ideas that obviously do not work?

It is time for us to re-evaluate all of our options.

The nation's focus has gone from rehabilitation to punishment because rehabilitation was not working. Perhaps, it is time for us to examine the reasons why the rehabilitation process was not working.

Anderson. © 1995 by Kirk Anderson. Reprinted with permission.

Many prisons have lost some of their programs in recent months, but most of our prisons offer basic education classes, GED classes, college courses, several vocational options, and many different types of therapy groups, such as AA [Alcoholics Anonymous], 12 Steps, anger control groups, sexual deviance groups, and others. You would think with all of these options, rehabilitation would be a viable solution, so what is the problem? The problem is that all of these programs are pretty much voluntary. Except in rare instances, inmates are not forced to utilize any of these options and many of them do not. When their time in prison is up, they are returning to society basically unchanged in their ability to cope and unable to become a productive member of their community.

The Future After Prison

Research has shown that a person who has advanced their education and received counseling while in prison is much less likely to return to prison than someone who has been idle during their incarceration. If a criminal is told upon entering prison that he stands no chance for release until he can show that he has advanced his education and received counseling for whatever problems led up to his incarceraton, then he will have a definite incentive to work toward self-improvement. When they achieve that, they will have no excuse for returning to prison. There will always be those who cannot be rehabilitated, but the vast majority can be.

Every criminal that is released from prison will be living in someone's neighborhood. Ask yourself this: which would you rather have living in your neighborhood: someone who has spent 20 years in prison without seeking any type of self-improvement or someone who has spent 10 years in prison that were geared toward education and counseling? Lengthy prison sentences do have their place in our system, but they are not the ultimate solution, and they should be kept in their place. If a person continually commits crimes, thereby showing that he has no intention of ever being a productive member of society, then that person should be removed from society, but cases should be judged on an individual basis.

There is no question that criminals must be punished, but our current system not only fails them . . . it fails us. In many ways, the average citizen is paying more for the crime than the criminal himself. The current trend would have us send a criminal to prison for a long period of time, say 20 years. During that time, we will pay for all maintenance on the prison, prisoner's food, clothes, medical care, dental needs, etc. . . . and at the end of that time, when the criminal is released, there is a strong possibility that he will act out against society again. On the other hand, at less cost than 20 years of idle time, we could send that same criminal to prison for 10 years and gear that time toward advancing formal education and counseling. Not only would it save tax dollars, it would greatly reduce the risk of that individual returning to prison.

Why should we continue to support a criminal justice system that is clearly failing, one that many times over costs the innocent more than the guilty?

It is time for us, as a nation, to demand that our representatives find an answer that works and to stop telling us what they think we want to hear. For a system geared, not toward long term incarceration for punishment, but toward shorter term incarceration with an emphasis on education and rehabilitation, could very well be the solution we are seeking.

Viewpoint 6

"Punishment through imprisonment is above all else an expression of our sense of justice and of the value our society places on freedom and on individual responsibility."

Prisons Should Punish Inmates

Charles H. Logan

In the following viewpoint, Charles H. Logan argues against the notion that prisons should rehabilitate prisoners. The philosophy of rehabilitation, in his opinion, is based on the mistaken belief that criminals are victims of social and personal deficiencies beyond their control. Instead, according to Logan, prisons should employ punitive measures in order to hold convicts personally accountable for their crimes. Logan is a professor and associate head of sociology at the University of Connecticut and the author of *Private Prisons: Cons and Pros*.

As you read, consider the following questions:

1. What prompts people to change their criminal behavior, according to Logan?
2. In the author's opinion, how might an emphasis on rehabilitation actually encourage crime?
3. What are the benefits of privatizing prisons, as stated by Logan?

Charles H. Logan, "Run Prisons Differently," *American Enterprise*, May/June 1995.

Prisons are the favorite whipping boy of every critic of the American criminal justice system. Some say we have too many of them, others too few. It is argued that prisons are too full, that they cost too much, that they have become too comfortable, or not comfortable enough. There are questions as to whether they rehabilitate, deter, or even incapacitate.

Some of these controversies would clear up if we had a better understanding of the practical and moral importance of prisons. Punishment through imprisonment is above all else an expression of our sense of justice and of the value our society places on freedom and on individual responsibility. Doing justice is the true mission of our prisons, and the single most important thing we can do to aid them is to purge them of any official responsibility for rehabilitation.

Blurring Accountability

Prisons should not try to be "correctional institutions." Changing behavior is not impossible—the majority of those released from prison do not return—but it happens only through self-restraint and individual reform. When we define rehabilitation as a collective responsibility to be achieved through the criminal justice system, the principle of accountability gets blurred.

The message of prison should be simple: "Felonies are wrong and controllable acts, and those who commit them will be punished." Institutions aiming for "rehabilitation" more often transmit this muddled message: "Felonies are the result of social and personal deficiencies (of opportunity, knowledge, skills, habits, temperament, and so on), and society has a responsibility to correct those deficiencies." That message depicts criminal behavior as uncontrollable rather than willful, and portrays offenders as automatons in need of adjustment rather than responsible human beings who must accept the consequences of their actions. Such a message may excuse, and even encourage, crime; at the very least, it weakens the vital punishment message of imprisonment.

"But," we are warned, "most prisoners will return to society eventually; don't we want them to come back prepared to lead noncriminal lives?" Indeed, we do. We not only want that, we demand it—but we demand it of the victimizer, not of the prison system. And in this we do not ask much: Do not hit, rob, rape, kill, swindle, or otherwise aggress against your fellow citizens. Those whom we send to prison, rather than to a mental hospital, already have all the equipment they need to refrain from crime. What they do with their lives beyond that is not the business of the penal system.

Prisons Should Not Be Comfortable

Prisons should not be comfortable for the inmates. The government, along with the sheriffs of the prisons, should work together to make sure the prisons are as uncomfortable as possible, so the inmates will not want to return. . . . Prisons are not supposed to be hotels; the living conditions should be as meager as possible.

Chandra M. Hayslett, University of Tennessee *Daily Beacon*, November 19, 1996.

So, how can we improve the effectiveness of prisons in curbing anti-social behavior and carrying out justice? For one thing, sentences need to be less rubbery. Most prisoners today have committed crimes that average citizens strongly believe should lead to imprisonment, and the specific sentences imposed generally reflect a broad consensus about the seriousness of various crimes. Once handed down, these sentences should be served in their entirety. To convey a clear message about the wrongness of crime, we need a system in which punishments are carried out fully as prescribed. When sentences get reduced sometime after sentencing for expedient reasons we end up with unfairness (as when a murderer ends up doing less time than a thief) and mixed signals to lawbreakers (as when a crime that is declared to deserve 10 years of loss of liberty actually only brings three years). Thus we need truth in sentencing: a requirement that all prisoners serve at least 85 percent of their sentence.

Prison Privatization

To meet the current level of serious crime in the United States we also need more prisons. We can afford this—prisons remain a small, if growing, portion of government spending. But we certainly don't want to waste money on them.

How can taxpayers tell if their government is giving them good value for their prison dollars? The best guarantee is to put the government in competition with the private sector.

As of June 1994, there were 84 private prison facilities with a total capacity of 43,508 beds under contract with various government bodies. A growing body of research demonstrates that these private prisons save money, improve quality, and protect inmates' rights, and that they produce no problems not already faced by governmental operations. Prison privatization has been called "controversial," but most of the resistance has been manufactured by dedicated opponents like public employee unions who feel threatened at the prospect of competition (as well they should). A decade of mostly positive experience has proven the value of private prisons.

Periodical Bibliography

The following articles have been selected to supplement the diverse views presented in this chapter.

Dan Baum	"Invisible Nation," *Rolling Stone*, December 7, 2000.
Pam Belluck	"As More Prisons Go Private, States Seek Tighter Controls," *New York Times*, April 15, 1999.
James Brooke	"In 'Super Max,' Terms of Endurance," *New York Times*, June 13, 1999.
Mark Frances Cohen	"Showdown with Sheriff Joe," *George*, December/January 2001.
David Cole	"Doing Time—In Rehab," *Nation*, September 20, 1999.
Ellis Cose	"The Prison Paradox," *Newsweek*, November 13, 2000.
John J. DiIulio Jr. and Joseph P. Tierney	"An Easy Ride for Felons on Probation," *New York Times*, August 29, 2000.
Gregory Frederick	"Prisoners Are Citizens," *Monthly Review*, July 2001.
John S. Goldkamp	"The Drug Court Response: Issues and Implications for Justice Change," *Albany Law Review*, Spring 2000.
Jennifer Gonnerman	"Two Million and Counting," *Village Voice*, February 22, 2000.
Sam Hine	"The Prison Boom: Corporate Profits, Human Losses," *Witness*, November 1998.
John Irwin, Vincent Schiraldi, and Jason Zeidenburg	"America's One Million Nonviolent Prisoners," *Social Justice*, Summer 2000.
Robert E. Moffit and David B. Mulhausen	"America's Prisons Are Full—of Criminals," *Human Events*, June 21, 2000.
Anamaria Wilson	"Lock 'em Up!" *Time*, February 14, 2000.

CHAPTER 3

Should Sentencing Laws Be Reformed?

Chapter Preface

Rising crime rates during the 1980s led many Americans to demand that their political leaders do something to control crime. Politicians quickly discovered that passing laws requiring a mandatory minimum sentence for certain crimes—such as drug offenses, weapons violations, and murder—was very popular with voters. With the passage of these federal and state mandatory sentencing laws, criminals could no longer count on the leniency of the judge or mitigating circumstances to reduce their sentence.

Advocates of mandatory minimum sentences stress that the sentences are fair: Different offenders convicted of the same offense serve the same amount of time in prison. Judges are not be able to reduce (or increase) the sentence because of the criminal's race, background, or gender. In addition, supporters contend that the tough sentences benefit society by taking criminals off the streets for lengthy periods. Others assert that the threat of lengthy prison terms serves as a powerful deterrent for other criminals.

But when thousands of nonviolent, small-time drug offenders were sentenced to lengthy prison terms, many ordinary Americans began to have second thoughts about mandatory minimums. Opponents of the mandatory sentencing laws charged that defendants convicted of using drugs for their own personal use were being sentenced to more time in prison (82.4 months) than criminals convicted of sexual assault (66.9 months), assault (33.4 months), manslaughter (26.8 months), burglary (24.6 months), and car theft (20 months). Many judges publicly lamented the fact that they were not able to adjust the sentence they were forced by law to impose to a sentence that was a more fair punishment for the crime. While Americans agree that criminals should be punished, they disagree on how severe the sentences should be. The authors in the following chapter examine this issue and others as they explore the topic of sentencing laws.

1

VIEWPOINT

"There is little evidence to suggest that the implementation of the 'three-strikes' law in California has had any significant impact on crime."

Three-Strikes Laws Should Be Reformed

Ryan S. King and Marc Mauer

Three-strikes laws impose severe imprisonment sentences on serious, habitual criminals who have been convicted of a second or third felony offense. In the following viewpoint, Ryan S. King and Marc Mauer argue that three-strikes laws are flawed and should be reformed. They reject the claim that three-strikes laws have led to a drop in crime rates, insisting that other factors such as an improved economy and improved policing have caused the decline. In addition, three-strikes laws often levy disproportionate punishment on criminals, some of whom are sent to prison for life for petty crimes such as stealing a candy bar. The law will have a significant impact on increasing the prison population, including the number of elderly prisoners, placing an extraordinary burden on the penal system. King is a research associate with The Sentencing Project; Mauer is assistant director of The Sentencing Project.

As you read, consider the following questions:

1. What percentage of repeat felons are sentenced under the three-strikes law for non-violent crimes?
2. What examples do the authors give of disproportionate sentences under the three-strikes law?

Ryan S. King and Marc Mauer, "Aging Behind Bars: 'Three-Strikes' Seven Years Later," *The Sentencing Project*, August 2001, pp. 6–7, 9–10, 13.

When the California "three strikes" law was enacted in 1994, Governor Pete Wilson sang the praises of the new initiative as a stern message to potential offenders. Attorney General Dan Lungren referred to the legislation as the "crown jewel" of a statewide assemblage of more uncompromising criminal justice laws.

The Rationale for "Three-Strikes"

At the time of the law's adoption, the Governor's Office contended that the "three strikes" policy would save the state anywhere from $140,000 to over $500,000 per repeat offender per year, far outpacing any potential rise in future criminal justice expenditures. Chief economist Phillip Romero concluded that by 2000–2001, there would be over 84,000 inmates in the California correctional system directly attributable to the "three strikes" legislation. Their incapacitation would provide a *social benefit* of $16.8 billion at a correctional cost of only $2.7 billion; an estimated cumulative savings for California taxpayers of $14.1 billion.

By 1996, California Youth and Adult Correctional Agency secretary Joseph Sandoval reported that in excess of "1,600 three-time felons with *serious or violent* (emphasis added) criminal histories, and nearly 16,700 two-time felons with similar backgrounds, have been taken off the streets because of this law." Attorney General Lungren noted that the drop in crime during 1994 (post-law) was nearly twice as steep as in 1993 (pre-law). Furthermore, three-quarters of the way through 1995, preliminary figures were showing a slightly larger drop in crime than had been seen in 1994. These numbers were convincing enough for Lungren, and most other supporters of "three strikes," to conclude that the legislation was operating to further suppress criminal activity independent of the overall general downward crime trend both in California and nationwide.

In a 1996 piece in *Policy Review*, Lungren made numerous claims that were designed to bolster opinion concerning the efficacy of "three strikes." Nearly five years have elapsed since publication of that article, and over seven years since California adopted the law. This report will evaluate how the promises (and myths) of "three strikes" have withstood the passage of time.

Myth: California is setting records for its crime drop

Lungren, in 1996, made the claim that within 18 months of the passage of "three strikes" legislation, California set records for the largest drop in state history in a number of categories of violent and property crime. He attributed this drop to the newly instituted habitual offender laws.

Fact: Crime has been on a consistent downturn both in California and nationally since the beginning of the 1990s. Leading criminologists view increased incarceration as but one factor among many that has contributed to the national declines. These include an improved economy, changes in drug markets, demographic changes, and strategic policing. During the "three strikes" era, 1993 to present, there was a national drop in crime of 22.2%, which was outpaced by a reduction of 41% in California. Although the crime drop in California was steeper than the national average, to make the sweeping generalization that "three strikes" provided the impetus for this requires further investigation. Recent analysis of both California and national data demonstrates that the decline in crime in California cannot be significantly attributed to the "three strikes" law.

Contrary to the conclusions of Lungren and others, criminologists Lisa Stoltzenberg and Stewart D'Alessio found that the decline in crime in California after 1994 merely continued existing trends that were unrelated to the law, and was not statistically significant. Their analysis of crime trends in the ten largest cities in California found that "three strikes" legislation did not diminish serious or minor crime beyond what would have been expected based on the existent downward trend. A state commissioned report produced similar findings, with the California Department of Justice's Criminal Justice Statistics Center stating that they could find no "valid evaluations" of "get tough" laws that were able to empirically verify that they exercise a direct negative effect on crime rates. . . .

Myth: "Three Strikes" is not Disproportionate Punishment

Lungren asserts that the way the law is designed does not levy unduly harsh punishment for minor offenses. Although there are occasions in which the third strike may be a minor felony, "there is nothing disproportionate about giving a harsh sentence to a felon who has not learned from having committed two serious felonies before."

Fact: If "three strikes" did function in the manner which Lungren describes, there would be less controversy about the policy. However, the California Department of Corrections reports that the majority of those sentenced under the repeat offender laws are sentenced for non-violent crimes. 57.9% of third strike cases are for property, drug, or other non-violent offenses, as are fully 69% of second strike cases. This is a major flaw in the operation of the habitual offender laws, and demonstrates that the law is not addressing the serious felons which Lungren promised.

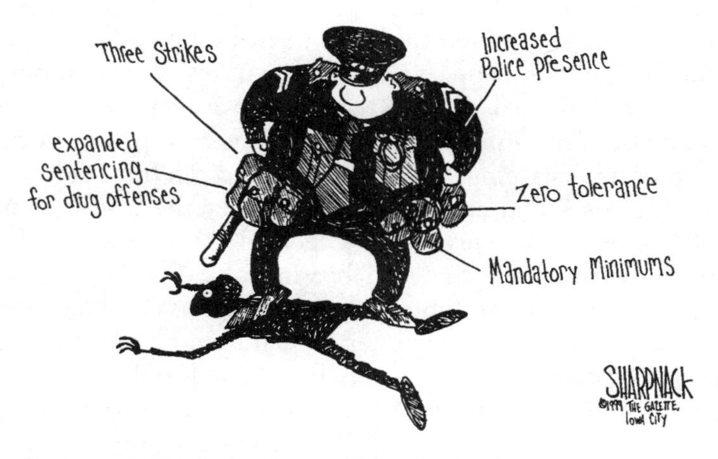

Sharpnack. © 1999 by Joe Sharpnack. Reprinted with permission.

"Three strikes" was described by its proponents as targeting the most violent career criminals and gained public favor in the wake of such heinous crimes as the Polly Klaas murder. However, an ever increasing number of "three strikes" prosecutions are for crimes as menial as petty theft of a can of beer or a few packs of batteries. This misdirected use of the law has led original crusader Mark Klaas to conclude that in its current manifestation, the "three strikes" laws are not working. "In the depth of despair which all Californians shared with my family immediately following Polly's murder, we blindly supported the [Reynolds] initiative in the mistaken belief that it dealt only with violent crimes. Instead, three of the four crimes it addresses are not violent."

Some of the more egregious applications of "three strikes" for property crime include the case of Scott Benscoter, a three striker serving 25 to life, who had two prior felony convictions for residential burglary when he was sentenced for the theft of a pair of sneakers. Or the case of Arthur Gibson, sentenced to 25 to life for crack possession, having last been convicted of a violent offense in the 1960s.

In July 1997, Gregory Taylor, a homeless Los Angeleno, was sentenced to 25 to life for trying to jimmy a church kitchen door. Taylor had received food from a priest there in the past and had apparently returned hoping to encounter that same priest. The case was appealed to the California Supreme Court, which declined to hear the case. And, in June 2000 a man's appeal of a "three strikes" conviction for the theft of $20 worth of instant coffee was denied.

The disparities produced by the exercise of prosecutorial discretion in charging "three strikes" cases can be seen by examining cases that are not charged under the law. In June 2000, San Francisco prosecutors decided not to seek 25 to life on Joey Trimm for the fatal beating of a four-month old puppy. Trimm, a two-time felon convicted for child molestation in 1990, beat the dog after he had found him eating cat food. The dog reacted by biting Trimm, and so Trimm retaliated by punching the animal and inflicting fatal wounds.

In the world of "three strike" sentencing, a homeless man simply looking for food is considered more of a consistent danger to society than a two-time child molester who has such poor impulse control that the sight of a puppy eating cat food is a catalyst to fatal violence. . . .

The Law's Effects

There is little evidence to suggest that the implementation of the "three strikes" law in California has had any significant impact on crime, but a good deal of evidence that demonstrates that it often results in disproportionate sentencing and will contribute substantially to the prison population over time.

In addition, the policy is already exacerbating the racial disparities that exist in the prison system. As is true nationally, African-Americans and Hispanics are disproportionately represented in the California penal system, comprising 31.3% and 34% of the inmate population respectively, compared to their respective shares of 7.5% and 31.6% in the general population. The impact of "three strikes" laws in California and other states has enhanced these disparities within the prison system for reasons that could have been readily foreseen at the time of the law's passage. In California, blacks make up 37% of those sentenced under second strike laws and 44% of those sentenced under third strike laws.

Similar effects have been produced in other states. In Washington State, although the law is used more sparingly, blacks are less than 4% of the population, but account for 37% of those sentenced under the "three strikes" law. The racial disparities produced by "three strikes" largely result from the fact that African-Americans have higher rates of arrest, and therefore prior convictions, than do whites. Whether due to greater involvement in crime or racial bias in the criminal justice system, the result is that minorities become more likely candidates for prosecution under habitual offender laws.

With crime declining nationally in the 1990s for a host of reasons, this is now an opportune moment to examine current sentencing policies and their consequences. As the state with the nation's largest prison population, California policymakers would be well served by considering whether "three strikes" is the most effective means of achieving public safety and fairness.

Policymakers in other states can learn from the California experience as well. Much of the critique of the "three strikes" policy also applies to rigid sentencing formulas such as mandatory sentencing and "truth in sentencing," both of which often result in lengthy and inappropriate incarceration. The public would be well served by a full examination of such policies and alternatives that would more effectively promote public safety.

2

VIEWPOINT

"A look back over the past 50 years shows that when habitual criminals are kept behind bars, the crime rate goes down."

Three-Strikes Laws Should Not Be Reformed

Part I: Robert Kelsey; Part II: Ted Westerman

In Part I of this two-part viewpoint, Robert Kelsey argues that the three-strikes law is doing what it was designed to do: incarcerate habitual felons so that they are no longer a menace to society. In Part II, Ted Westerman contends that the criminals sentenced under the three-strikes laws have committed a second or third violent or serious felony and therefore deserve a severe sentence. In addition, he asserts that the three-strikes law is responsible for a declining crime rate. Kelsey is a retired deputy probation officer in California; Westerman is chairman of the Criminal Justice Legal Foundation in Sacramento.

As you read, consider the following questions:

1. According to Kelsey, why are counties that ignore third strikes still experiencing a drop in crime rates?
2. By how much did the California crime rate decline since the passage of the three-strikes law, as cited by Kelsey?
3. According to Westerman, how does California's crime rate compare to the rest of the nation?

I

A *North [San Diego] County Times* editorial supports a doctoral student's incredible contention that incarceration of 40,000 habitual criminals under the "three-strikes" law has had "no effect on crime."

The student, Mike Males of the University of California, Irvine, acknowledged that crime is declining statewide, but says it has nothing to do with three strikes, because counties that do not vigorously enforce the third strike are experiencing the same decline as other counties.

Males and the *North County Times* lament that drug and property-crime offenders comprise two-thirds of those imprisoned on a third strike. Males calls them "nuisances, not menaces," despite their histories of serious or violent felony convictions. Joining in the sympathy, the *Times* referred to a drug crime as a "personal habit," and at the same time endorsed the amendment of three strikes to require a violent felony for the third strike "to ensure that people who could be productive members of society are not swept away forever with the violent and the incurable."

Really? Habitual felons stealing and using dope are good candidates to become productive members of society? Do habitual criminals become more benign when they are on drugs, or do they become more dangerous?

The Truth Behind Chronic Offenders

The editorial shows a lack of knowledge of the traits and behavior patterns of chronic offenders, the three-strikes law, and crime in general. Here is a more complete picture:

- Three strikes is designed to put habitual criminals away as quickly as possible to protect the public. Any felony is its trigger mechanism for 25 years to life. It is the last straw. Why wait for the big crime that is almost certain to happen?
- Only a small percentage of offenders convicted under the three-strikes law are serving on a third strike. Most are serving time on a second conviction, which doubles the sentence, mandates consecutive sentences on separate counts and requires offenders to serve 80 percent of their time rather than 50 percent. In short, second strikers are serving a lot of time. This is very likely the reason why counties that wink at the

third strike are experiencing the same drop in crime as other counties. Their two-strikers are still in the slammer.

• The Justice Department reports that crime costs Americans $450 billion a year, and this excludes the cost of running the nation's prisons, jails, parole and probation systems, which together was $40 billion. A Rand Corp. survey of 2,190 offenders in three states found the average number of crimes committed by criminals in the study ranged from 187 to 287 a year. Taking the low end, they calculated the typical offender in the survey was responsible for $430,000 in crime costs. The cost to imprison each offender for a year was $25,000.

• Statewide, crime dropped 40 percent since the passage of three strikes.

Do we want to change something that is working and saving lives? Wouldn't it be better to consult with law enforcement and victims' organizations? I think so, because it appears the *Times* has linked arms with armchair academics, who traditionally have been the criminal's friend, at the expense of the public, and whose knowledge of crime and criminals seldom exceeds what one might learn in a sociology 101 textbook.

II

One apparent result of 1998's election has been to energize an effort to abandon the three-strikes sentencing of habitual criminals. Debate about the law has intensified during the 1999 legislative session. California Gov. Gray Davis vetoed one measure that would have provided alternatives to confinement for certain criminals. . . .

Misrepresentations

In news stories, opponents often misrepresent how three-strikes is being enforced and its effect on crime. For example:

Claim: The majority of criminals sentenced under the three-strikes law have been convicted of nonviolent crimes, like marijuana possession or petty theft.

Fact: In order to receive a three-strikes sentence, a criminal must be convicted of a second violent or serious felony. Violent felonies include crimes like murder, rape, armed robbery, aggravated assault and arson. Serious felonies include furnishing or selling drugs to children, residential burglary, carjacking and strong-armed robbery. A criminal who has earned a second strike receives at least double the prison term he received for the first conviction. For example, the sentence for forcible rape is six years. A second rape conviction would carry a minimum of 12 years. A person with two prior violent or serious felony convictions who commits a third felony can qualify for a third-strike sentence of 25 years to life. Petty theft and possession of marijuana for personal use are misdemeanors, not felonies.

Second and Third Strikers in California Prisons as of September 30, 2002

Offense Category	Number of 3rd Strikers	Number of 2nd Strikers
Crimes Against Persons (Homicide, robbery, assault, sexual offenses, kidnapping)	3,408	11,517
Property Crimes (Burglary, grand theft, petty theft, receiving stolen property, forgery/fraud)	2,240	10,933
Drug Crimes	1,276	9,785
Other Crimes (Escape, driving under the influence, arson, possession of weapon, and other)	615	3,186
Total:	7,539	35,421

State of California Department of Corrections, "Second and Third Strikers in the Institution Population," September 30, 2002.

When the three-strikes law was adopted in 1994, a person with two prior violent or serious felony convictions who was convicted for a second time of petty theft did qualify for the third strike. In 1996, the California Supreme Court held that trial judges have the discretion to ignore any prior convictions they determined would unjustly qualify the criminal for the 25-to-life sentence. Because few criminals specialize in only violent crimes, the majority of those going to prison under the three-strikes law are professional felons. Many have committed violent crimes in the past and, if surprised or confronted, would do so again.

The Decline in Crime

Claim: No evidence links the three-strikes law to the decline in crime.

Fact: Since adoption of three-strikes, California has outpaced the national drop in violent crime by 26.7%. The state's homicide rate has plummeted to the level it was in 1966, and violent crime is down one-third since 1994. This has been especially important to people living in the state's larger cities. People living in Detroit, a city with one-third the population of Los Angeles, suffer twice the rate of murder and rape of Angelenos.

Claim: Three-strikes enforcement will tie up billions of taxpayers' dollars for decades to come. Each prisoner serving a 25-to-life sentence will cost the state about $500,000 over his or her lifetime.

Fact: University of Chicago economist Steven Levitt estimates the savings in crime costs by keeping one habitual criminal in prison at $53,900 per year. That's $1,347,500 over 25 years that will not be spent—leaving $847,500 left for education and crime prevention programs after paying the cost of imprisonment. And can you even put a dollar value on murder, rape or burglary?

Claim: With second- and third-strikers flooding our prisons, other serious offenders are securing early release.

Fact: California prisons are not releasing anyone early because of the three-strikes law. Initially, some county jails were giving early releases to some nonviolent offenders, but this has subsided over the past three years.

Repeat Offenders Are Targeted

The key to three strikes and similar sentencing laws is that they target repeat felons. Because criminals face only a 1-in-12 chance of being arrested for each crime they commit, most have actually committed scores of serious crimes by the time they are convicted of a third felony. Should we go easy on the criminal with two prior convictions for rape because his most recent felony is for drug dealing?

A look back over the past 50 years shows that when habitual criminals are kept behind bars, the crime rate goes down. When that policy is weakened or abandoned, the crime rate goes up. More than 120,000 fewer men, women and children have become victims of murder, violent assault or rape in California since the three-strikes law was adopted. There have also been 450,000 fewer homes burglarized, 339,000 fewer cars stolen, and more than 170,000 fewer robberies. Weakening the three-strikes law would put a higher value on the interests of three-time felons than on the safety of thousands of innocent Californians. This is hardly the wise path to a safer California.

3

VIEWPOINT

"Capital punishment, the ultimate denial of civil liberties, is a costly, irreversible and barbaric practice, the epitome of cruel and unusual punishment."

Capital Punishment Should Be Abolished

American Civil Liberties Union

In the following viewpoint, the American Civil Liberties Union (ACLU) argues that the death penalty is a barbaric practice that does not deter crime. In addition, the organization asserts that the death penalty is not administered fairly; studies have found that the defendant's race, geographic location, and economic status greatly influence whether or not capital punishment is imposed. Furthermore, most civilized societies have given up requiring an eye-for-an-eye style of retribution. Therefore, the ACLU concludes, the death penalty should be abolished in the United States.

As you read, consider the following questions:

1. According to the author, how many people have been executed by the state since the death penalty was reinstated?
2. How many hours does a lawyer spend defending a death-penalty case, as cited by the ACLU?
3. What is the most important factor in levying the death penalty against a convicted murderer, according to the ACLU?

American Civil Liberties Union, "The Death Penalty," *ACLU Briefing Paper*, 1999.

The United States is on an execution rampage. Since capital punishment was reinstated by the Supreme Court in the 1976 *Gregg v. Georgia* decision, more than 525 men and women have been put to death by the state. More than 150 of these executions have taken place since 1996. 3,500 people are on death row today, awaiting their turn with the executioner.

Capital punishment has existed throughout most of the course of our nation's history. By the mid-1960s, however, public opposition to the death penalty had reached an all-time high, and the practice was banned by the Supreme Court in the 1972 *Furman v. Georgia* decision. The Court held that state death penalty statutes were devoid of any standards, and that they therefore gave too much discretion to individual judges and juries to exact the ultimate punishment.

Soon after the *Furman* decision, states began passing new laws that provided sentencing guidelines for juries. The Supreme Court was given another opportunity to address the issue of capital punishment in 1976, in *Gregg v. Georgia*, and it ruled that "the punishment of death does not invariably violate the Constitution." Since this ruling, capital punishment rates have grown exponentially in the United States.

In 1994, the Federal Death Penalty Act authorized capital punishment for more than 60 offenses, including some crimes that do not involve murder. Moreover, the 1996 Anti-Terrorism and Effective Death Penalty Act created new barriers to effective federal review of constitutional claims in capital cases. Congress and many states have also slashed funding for most of the legal representation death row inmates formerly received from death penalty resource centers.

Capital punishment, the ultimate denial of civil liberties, is a costly, irreversible and barbaric practice, the epitome of cruel and unusual punishment. It does not deter crime, and the way it is implemented is grotesquely unfair.

The Death Penalty Is Unfair

Regardless of one's viewpoint about the morality or constitutionality of the death penalty, most people would agree that if we are going to continue executing people in the U.S., we should be doing it fairly and rationally. However, three factors, unrelated to the crime itself, greatly influence who gets executed and who does not: poverty, race and geography.

Lethal Injection for the Poor

The American Bar Association and many scholars have found that what most often determines whether or not a death sentence is handed down is not the facts of the crime, but the quality of the legal representation. The overwhelming majority of death row inmates receive substandard legal representation at trial. Almost all capital-crime defendants are indigent when arrested, and are generally represented by court-appointed lawyers, who are inexperienced and underpaid. The *National Law Journal*, reviewing capital cases in six Southern states, reported that defense lawyers are often "ill-trained, unprepared. . . [and] grossly underpaid."

Defending a capital case is time-consuming, taking about 700–1000 hours. In some jurisdictions the hourly rates for appointed attorneys in capital cases are less than the minimum wage, and usually much less than the lawyer's hourly expenses. Moreover, courts often authorize inadequate funds for investigation and experts—or refuse to do so altogether. This is in the face of the almost limitless such funding for the prosecution. Wealthy people who can hire their own counsel are generally spared the death penalty, no matter how heinous their crimes. Poor people do not have the same oppurtunity to buy their lives.

Racial Bias Permeates the System

Death row in the U.S. has always held a disproportionately large population of people of color relative to the general population. Whereas African Americans constitute 12% of the U.S. population, they are 35% of those on death row; 9% are Native American, Latino or Asian. The most important factor in levying the death penalty, however, is the race of the victim. (Those who kill a white person are more likely to receive the death penalty than those who kill a black person.)

A 1998 report by the Death Penalty Information Center summarizes the findings of several scholars which illustrate this point. In 96% of the studies examining the relationship between race and the death penalty there was a pattern of race-of-victim or race-of-defendant discrimination, or both.

The report also reveals a consistent trend indicating race-of-victim discrimination. For example, in Florida, in comparable cases, "a defendant's odds of receiving a death sentence are 4.8 times higher if the victim was white than if the victim was black. In Illinois the multiplier is 4, in Oklahoma it is 4.3, in North Carolina, 4.4, and in Mississippi, it is 5.5."

The state of Kentucky presents a particularly outrageous example of race-of-victim discrimination: despite the fact that 1,000 African Americans have been murdered there since the 1975 reinstitution of the death penalty in that state, as of spring 1999, *all* of the state's 39 death row inmates were sentenced for murdering a white victim; none were there for murdering an African American.

Several studies show the effects of outright racial discrimination. One recent example, a 1998 University of Iowa study of sentencing in Philadelphia, showed that the odds of receiving a death sentence are nearly 3.9 times greater if the defendant is African American.

These patterns of racial disparities are partly explained by the fact that the nation's prosecutors, who make the threshold decision about whether or not to seek the death penalty are almost exclusively white men. Of the district attorneys in U.S. counties using capital punishment, 98% are white, and only 1% are African American. New York State has *only one* African American district attorney.

Where You Live Determines Whether You Die

Whether someone convicted of a capital crime receives a death sentence depends greatly on the state or county in which the trial and conviction takes place. In some states, a death sentence is rare. Connecticut had five people on death row in 1999; Kansas, only two. Southern states, particularly Texas (443 death row inmates in 1999), hand down significantly more death sentences than those in the rest of the country. California, the state with the largest penal system, had 513 inmates on death row in the spring of 1999. Such state-to-state disparities exist because death penalty statutes are a patchwork of disparate standards, rules and practices and the consequence is the difference between life and death. Furthermore, some prosecutors are more zealous in seeking the death penalty than others—particularly if they are running for re-election.

In some states, inmates can be executed for crimes they committed at the age of 16; in others, only those who committed murder at age 18 or older are eligible for the death penalty. Some states, but not all, ban the execution of people with mental retardation. Some states include felony murder (unpremeditated murder committed in the course of another crime such as robbery or burglary) as a capital crime; others do not. In the 29 states that have a sentence of life without parole, 23 have statutes that bar judges from letting jurors know they have that sentencing option. Since studies consistently show that when given a choice between a death sentence and a sentence of life without parole, most people will choose the latter, failure to inform a jury of this alternative is tantamount to sending more people to the execution chamber.

The Death Penalty Does Not Deter Crime

Murder is not a rational act done by rational people who carefully think through the consequences of their actions. Those who murder are usually either consumed by hate or anger or are in a warped emotional state. They are demented, pathological people who, at the time they kill, do so with utter disregard for human life. Many are either high on drugs or in desperate need for more drugs. Killers are by and large anti-social people who do not respond to such behavioral disincentives not to kill as the death penalty. Acceptance of normal societal values is alien to their individual natures. In my view, for us to think that we can influence or deter them from killing through capital punishment is in and of itself irrational thought and behavior.

James McCloskey, *Criminal Justice Ethics*, Winter/Spring 1996.

Social science research has discredited the claim that execution deters murder. The majority of murders are committed in the heat of passion, and/or under the influence of alcohol or drugs, when there is little thought given to the possible consequences of the act. "Hit men" and other murderers who plan their crimes beforehand, intend and expect to avoid punishment altogether by not getting caught.

Law enforcement officials know that the death penalty is not a deterrent. Imposing the death penalty more often was thought to be cost-effective by only 29% of 386 randomly selected U.S. police chiefs polled by Peter D. Hart Research Associates in 1995. States that have death penalty laws do not have lower crime rates or murder rates than states without such laws. And states that have abolished capital punishment, or reinstituted it, show no significant changes in either crime or murder rates.

An Unjustified and Irreversible Means of Retribution

However satisfying vengeance may seem, a civilized society cannot accept an eye-for-an-eye, tooth-for-a-tooth delivery of justice. Although some families and loved ones of murder victims approve the death penalty, many others are against it. Further, some family members of homicide victims comment that the death penalty process prolongs their pain, and only serves to make their healing more elusive.

Financial and emotional support is what they need most, not more violence. In the words of the father of one murder victim, "Violence is not an acceptable method of solving the problems that arise in our daily lives. . . . The use of the death penalty only lowers the standards of government to the mentality of the murderer himself." We do not punish rape with rape, or burn down the house of an arsonist. We should not, therefore, punish the murderer with death.

The irreversibility of the death penalty is especially significant in light of the percentage of innocent people on death row. A study published in 1982 in the *Stanford Law Review* documents 350 capital convictions in which it was later proven that the convict had not committed the crime. Of those, 23 convicts were executed; others spent decades of their lives in prison. In a 1996 update of this study it was revealed that in the past few years alone, four individuals were executed although there was strong evidence that they were not guilty of the crime for which they were condemned.

Since 1976, 77 persons have been released from death row because they were not guilty of the crime for which they had been condemned to death (33 of these releases have occurred since 1990). These lucky interventions occurred almost always as the result of the efforts of students, journalists or *pro bono* lawyers, often only hours before a scheduled execution, and usually after the condemned had been on death row for over ten years.

Although it is commonly thought that the death penalty is reserved for those who commit the most heinous crimes, in reality only a small percentage of death-sentenced inmates were convicted of unusually vicious crimes. The vast majority of individuals facing execution were convicted of crimes that are indistinguishable from crimes committed by others who are serving prison sentences, crimes such as murder committed in the course of an armed robbery.

A Barbaric Practice

Our nation exacts capital punishment in five ways: by hanging, electrocution, gas chamber, firing squad (still authorized in Idaho and Utah), and the most common method, lethal injection. The United States is the only Western industrialized nation that practices the death penalty, and is by far the nation with the largest death row roster in the world. In comparison, all of Western Europe has abolished the death penalty, either by decree of law, or by practice. Fifty-seven nations and territories outlaw the death penalty for any crime, fifteen more allow it only for exceptional crimes such as military law or wartime crimes. Another twenty-six countries and territories are abolitionist de facto, meaning they have not executed anyone during the past ten years or more, or that they have made an international commitment not to carry out executions. In numbers of people executed annually, the United States far exceeds the other 94 documented countries and territories that continue to deliver the death penalty.

Various polls of public attitudes about crime and punishment found that a majority of people in the United States support alternatives to capital punishment. According to the Death Penalty Information Center, when presented with possible sentencing alternatives, 50% of those surveyed chose life imprisonment without parole plus restitution to the victim's family as an alternative to the death penalty.

In 45 states, laws allow life sentences for murder that severely limit or eliminate the possibility of parole. Thirteen states impose sentences without the possibility of parole for 25–40 years, and all but three of the states that use capital punishment also have the option of life imprisonment with no possibility of parole. Although it is often assumed that capital punishment is less costly than life imprisonment, the opposite is true: in terms of dollars, in terms of crime control, and in terms of morality.

4

VIEWPOINT

"Executing people for murder deters other people from committing other murders."

Capital Punishment Should Not Be Abolished

William Tucker

In the following viewpoint, William Tucker contends that the death penalty deters crime and therefore should not be abolished. He cites studies that found that as the execution rate increased, the homicide rate decreased. In addition, states that impose capital punishment have lower homicide rates than states that do not have the death penalty—and the homicide rate continues to decline as the number of executed murderers increases. He concludes that the death penalty is a successful social policy that achieves its desired results. Tucker is a freelance writer in New York.

As you read, consider the following questions:

1. What happened to the U.S. homicide rate between 1963 and 1972, two years after the death penalty was abolished, according to Tucker?
2. What three categories should states be placed into regarding the death penalty, in the author's opinion?
3. How does Tucker characterize states without capital punishment?

William Tucker, "Capital Punishment Works," *Weekly Standard*, August 13, 2001, pp. 27–29.

Executing people for murder deters other people from committing other murders. Common sense would suggest to anyone that such a deterrent effect must exist. After all, people do fear losing their lives. And based on the evidence, it's hard to see why anyone would doubt the deterrent effect of the death penalty. Murder rates, which had trended downward since 1935, took off almost vertically after 1963, the year the Supreme Court started overturning state death penalty convictions on a routine basis. With capital punishment in abeyance, homicides rapidly climbed to unprecedented heights. From 4.9 per 100,000 in 1963, they doubled to 10.1 per 100,000 in 1972, two years after the Supreme Court finally overturned all existing capital punishment statutes. The national homicide rate reached a peak of 10.7 per 100,000 in 1980. And after a decade of dalliance when states condemned over 2,000 to death but executed only a handful, the rate was still at 10.5 per 100,000 in 1991.

Executions and Homicides

By the beginning of the 1990s, however, states that wished to reimpose the ultimate penalty had fought their way through the endless thicket of appeals and restrictions imposed by the courts. In 1991, 14 murderers were executed while 2,500 waited on death row. By 1993 the figure had risen to 38 executions, then 55 in 1995, and 98 in 1999, a level not seen since the 1950s. (The all-time high of 200 executions occurred in 1935.) At the same time, murder rates began to plummet—to 9.6 per 100,000 in 1993, 7.7 in 1996, and 6.4 in 1999, the lowest level since 1966. To put the matter simply, over the past 40 years, homicides have gone up when executions have gone down and vice versa.

Does this constitute proof of deterrence? Not a chance, say the critics. There's no evidence of cause and effect. Dozens of other factors could explain these numbers. The decline might be just a coincidence.

The same, of course, can be said of all statistical correlations. All the potential factors must be separated out before anyone can draw conclusions. The only way to obtain proof would be to conduct a social experiment. (Ernest van den Haag, a supporter of the death penalty, once suggested executing people only for murders committed on Monday, Wednesday, and Friday, to see if there would be any migration of violent crime to other days of the week.) But such experiments would be completely unethical.

State-by-State Analysis

The closest thing to this kind of experimentation that we have is the laboratory of the states—the differing death penalty regimes of the 50 states. And indeed, much attention has been lavished on the state-by-state figures, with the usual conclusion being that there is no deterrent effect from capital punishment, or even that executions may have a reverse effect. "Death-penalty states as a group do not have lower rates of criminal homicide than non-death-penalty states," says the American Civil Liberties Union (ACLU). "During the 1970s death-penalty states averaged an annual rate of 7.9 criminal homicides per 100,000 population; abolitionist states averaged a rate of 5.1."

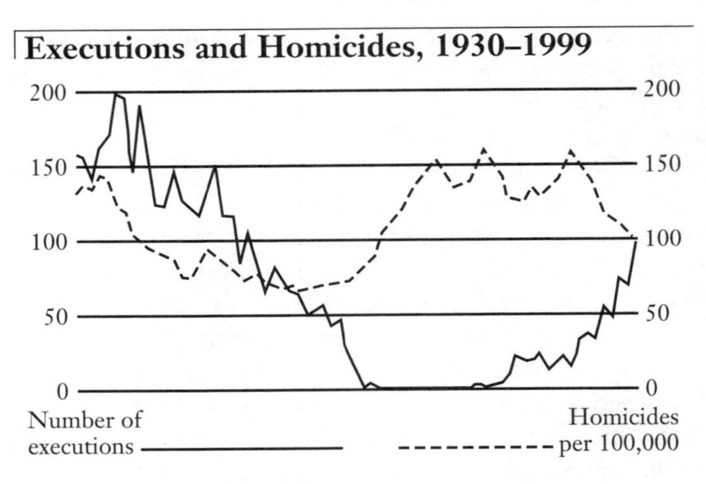

William Tucker, *Weekly Standard*, August 13, 2001.

In September 2000, the *New York Times* announced on the front page that its own survey had reached identical conclusions. "In a state-by-state analysis," said the report, "the *Times* found that during the last 20 years, the homicide rate in states with the death penalty has been 48 percent to 101 percent higher than in states without the death penalty. . . . Indeed, 10 of the 12 states without capital punishment have homicide rates below the national average, . . . while half the states with the death penalty have homicide rates above the national average . . . suggesting to many experts that the threat of the death penalty rarely deters criminals." Indeed, the figures might even support the allegations of some death penalty opponents that capital punishment *encourages* murder. After all, barbarity begets barbarity.

The *Times* study is not as definitive as it may have appeared, however. It used figures only through 1996, even though 1998 numbers were available. (The ACLU, which lists execution-versus-murder-rate statistics on its website to prove "Capital Punishment is Not a Deterrent to Murder," stopped counting in 1995.) And the graph that accompanied the article seemed to show homicide rates falling a lot faster in states with capital punishment than without. Finally, the *Times* decided to leave New York and Kansas out of its survey, because these two states had adopted the death penalty only in the 1990s. New York's tumbling rate of crime would have had a considerable effect on the results obtained. But those are the choices involved in any survey.

The important thing is that, as crime statistics from the years subsequent to the ACLU and *New York Times* research have unfolded, a very interesting pattern has emerged: States with death penalties indeed started with historically higher rates of murder. But since 1994, murder rates in these states have fallen significantly, so that the gap between the two groups has been more than cut in half. If current trends continue, the divergence will disappear altogether.

Three Categories of States

This pattern can be seen most clearly if you put the states into three categories instead of the *Times*'s two: (1) states that execute people for murder; (2) states that have adopted a death penalty but have not executed anyone, and (3) states that have no death penalty. (This solves the problem of New York and Kansas, which fall neatly into the second category.) At the beginning of the decade, the three groups ranked in that order, top to bottom, in their rate of homicide. Murder rates in states that execute people were twice as high as in states without capital punishment, while states with capital punishment that have not yet executed anyone fell almost exactly in the middle. This would suggest that a state's decision on whether to adopt and implement capital punishment was influenced by how serious the problem of murder was perceived to be.

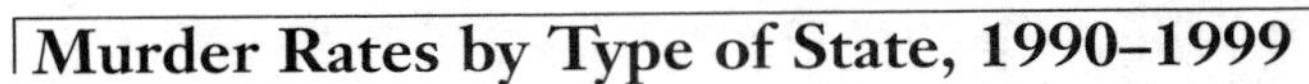

Murder Rates by Type of State, 1990–1999

Note: The figures in the graphic above were arrived at by averaging the homicide rates of the states in each group. This could be seen as unrepresentative. As in the U.S. Senate, a homicide rate in New York (population, 18.9 million) is weighed just as heavily as that in Delaware (783,000). Yet weighing the murder rates by population drowns the results from the smaller states and creates a figure determined only by a few large states. Since each state is, in effect, a separate experiment in the effects of capital punishment, it is more appropriate to weigh each state equally. The District of Columbia—a single city (572,000) with a murder rate almost ten times the national average and higher than anywhere in the world except South Africa—is not included. When District figures are averaged with the states lacking a death penalty, the line for jurisdictions without capital punishment is almost the same as the line for states that have capital punishment but no executions. Neither the New York Times *nor the ACLU includes the District of Columbia in its surveys.*

William Tucker, *Weekly Standard*, August 13, 2001.

Homicide rates have since fallen steadily in states that have performed executions, with the downward arc beginning in 1994. States with capital punishment but no executions have lowered their homicide rate but in a more uneven pattern. States with no capital punishment saw a slight decline that was almost completely wiped out by an upswing in 1999. Almost the entire drop in murder rates over the past decade has occurred in states with capital punishment, with the biggest decrease seen in states that are executing people.

States without capital punishment are generally liberal Democratic strongholds—Maine, Vermont, Massachusetts, Rhode Island, West Virginia, Michigan, Minnesota, Iowa, North Dakota, and Hawaii. Wisconsin and Alaska also have no death penalty. One feature that most share is a cold climate. "The best policeman in the world is a cold night" is an old law-enforcement adage, and states with severe winters have traditionally had lower crime rates. All of these states (except Michigan) also have relatively small African-American populations. Since African Americans commit murder at six times the rate of other population groups, this is likely to produce lower murder rates.

States with capital punishment that have not yet executed anyone tend to be states with liberal politics and large minority populations. New York, New Jersey, Connecticut, and New Mexico are representative. (The others are New Hampshire, Kansas, and South Dakota.) Combined, these states have only 27 people on death row and have not executed anyone. Often this is as much a reflection of jury decisions as state policies. In Connecticut, for example, a jury recently refused to impose the death penalty on a 25-year-old drug dealer, already serving a 35-year sentence, who had ordered the execution of a woman and her 8-year-old son because the boy had witnessed the murder of his mother's boyfriend, for which the drug dealer's brother was being tried. Although this heinous crime sparked a revision of the state's witness protection program, the jury did not see fit to impose the death penalty.

Thirty-one states now have capital punishment and are performing executions. They are scattered across the map but tend to be concentrated in the South. Texas, Missouri,

Oklahoma, Louisiana, Florida, Georgia, and Virginia have performed the majority of the nation's executions although Pennsylvania, Ohio, Montana, Idaho, Oregon, and Washington have had them as well. Generally these southern states have hot weather and large African-American populations, both of which have traditionally contributed to a higher murder rate.

Texas has had the highest number of executions (216 since 1990) and is constantly berated for it. Yet the results have been striking. In 1991, the state's murder rate was 15.3 per 100,000, second in the nation only to Louisiana. By 1999, it had fallen to 6.1, below 19 other states and close to the national average of 5.7. Florida (fourth in executions since 1990) has reduced its murder rate from 10.7 to 5.7. By contrast, non-executing New Mexico, with a similar climate and demographic profile, started the decade with a rate of 9.2 per 100,000 and ended with 9.8. Among the 31 states with executions, only four had a higher rate of murder at the end of the decade than at the beginning. Among the seven states with capital punishment but no executions, three finished with a higher rate of murder, while among the 12 states without capital punishment, five did.

A Deterrent Effect

More sophisticated evidence of deterrence is also emerging. In 1976, Isaac Ehrlich, a University of Chicago researcher in econometrics, studied month-by-month patterns of murder and executions from data extending back into the 1930s. He found a deterrent effect of about eight murders for every execution. Ehrlich's study was introduced in evidence before the Supreme Court when it reversed its moratorium on executions in 1976, but the paper has since been subject to endless challenge and alleged refutation. In any case, the data are now outdated.

In May of this year, Hashem Dezhbakhsh, Paul Rubin, and Joanna Shepherd, three Emory University economists, published an updated version of Ehrlich's analysis using county-by-county data gathered since the renewal of executions. "Our results suggest the legal change allowing executions beginning in 1977 has been associated with significant reductions in homicide," they conclude. "In particular, the execution of each offender seems to save, on average, the lives of 18 potential victims." The authors estimate a margin of error of plus-or-minus 10, meaning as many as 28 but no less than 8 potential victims are saved with each execution.

This solid evidence of a deterrent effect should become a part of the death penalty debate. Whether it is wrong to execute people who are retarded, whether the indigent get sufficient legal counsel, whether African Americans are over- or underrepresented on death row, the role of DNA evidence in death-row cases—all these are questions to be debated on their merits. To date, however, opponents of the death penalty have all too often simply asserted that capital punishment has been proved to lack a deterrent effect. This of course means that defenders of the death penalty get cast as defenders of some barbaric ritual—as if they were in favor of sacrificing a virgin in the springtime in order to ensure a good harvest.

To the contrary, capital punishment is a social policy that achieves targeted results. Its very success is what now allows people to talk about some of its secondary aspects in a tranquil environment. With murders down nearly 40 percent since 1991, public alarm has abated. Those who would use this opportunity to abolish capital punishment must reckon with the innocent lives that will be lost if they succeed.

5

VIEWPOINT

"Two decades after the enactment of mandatory sentences, these laws have failed to deter people from using or selling drugs."

Mandatory Minimum Sentences Are Ineffective in the War Against Drugs

Families Against Mandatory Minimums

Mandatory minimum sentencing laws require judges to impose fixed sentences for particular crimes, usually drug infractions. In the following viewpoint, Families Against Mandatory Minimums (FAMM), an organization dedicated to reforming the mandatory minimum sentencing laws, argues that inflexible mandatory minimum sentences are excessive and are used too frequently against low-level, nonviolent drug offenders. The safety valve provisions, which are supposed to prevent these small-time drug offenders from receiving excessively harsh sentences, are too narrowly drawn to help them, FAMM asserts. The organization maintains that mandatory minimums, which were designed to deter people from engaging in illegal drug activity, have very little effect in the war on drugs.

As you read, consider the following questions:

1. Which two states have the strictest mandatory minimum sentencing laws, according to FAMM?
2. What two factors primarily determine the sentence length imposed on a drug offender, as cited by the author?
3. In FAMM's opinion, why are there more low-level drug offenders in prison than high-level drug traffickers?

A confidential informant approached Joseph Settembrino, 18, about selling LSD. Between jobs and needing money for a car payment, Settembrino negotiated to sell LSD to two friends. Though he had never been in trouble with the law, Settembrino received a 10-year federal mandatory sentence.

Brenda Valencia's aunt didn't have a driver's license, so Valencia gave her ride. Unfortunately, it was to a house where the aunt sold seven kilos of cocaine. Though Valencia knew nothing of the sale, a cocaine dealer cooperating with the prosecution for a lower sentence testified that she did. She received a 10-year mandatory sentence, plus two years because her aunt had carried a concealed weapon. The sentencing judge said, "This case is the perfect example of why the minimum mandatory sentences and the sentencing guidelines are not only absurd, but an insult to justice. This young lady does not need to be sentenced to 151 months without parole; however, the law is the law, and we're all bound to obey it. But it's absolutely ridiculous to impose this sentence in this case, considering the degree of participation that this defendant had in the crime."

On a tip from a confidential informant, police raided Lance Marrow's apartment, found drugs and arrested both Marrow and his roommate. The bags containing crack and powder cocaine residue belonged to the roommate; only a dollar bill with powder cocaine on it was Lance's. Lance did not know that drugs were in his apartment. Convinced of his innocence, Lance went to trial, where, at the age of 50, he was convicted and sentenced under New York's Rockefeller drug laws to a mandatory state term of 15 years to life.

Settembrino, Valencia, Marrow and tens of thousands of low-level, non-violent drug offenders have learned a hard lesson about federal and state mandatory sentencing laws: judges have no discretion to fit the punishment to the crime or the individual. Indeed, most people know nothing about mandatory sentencing laws until they are personally affected.

What Are Mandatory Sentences?

The American justice system traditionally permits judges to weigh all the facts of a case when determining an offender's sentence. But in the 1970s and 1980s, the U.S. Congress and many state legislatures passed laws that force judges to give fixed prison terms to those convicted of specific crimes, most often drug offenses. Members of Congress and state legislators believed these harsh, inflexible sentences would catch those at the top of the drug trade and deter others from entering it.

Instead, this heavy-handed response to the nation's drug problem filled prisons with low-level offenders, resulting in over-capacity prison populations and higher costs for taxpayers. Mandatory sentencing laws disproportionately affect people of color and, because of their severity, destroy families. Two decades after the enactment of mandatory sentences, these laws have failed to deter people from using or selling drugs: drugs are cheaper, purer and more easily obtainable than ever before.

On these pages you'll learn about federal and state sentencing laws and the six major problems that arise with mandatory sentences for drugs and other offenses:

1. Judges can't consider the facts of each case.
2. The type and weight of a drug primarily determines sentence length.
3. They remove checks and balances.
4. They encourage and reward those who inform on others.
5. Conspiracy laws make those at the top of the drug trade and low-level offenders equally culpable.
6. Low-level offenders often get longer sentences than high-level dealers.

Federal Sentences

There are two types of federal sentencing laws: mandatory minimum sentencing laws, enacted by Congress, and the sentencing guidelines, enacted by the United States Sentencing Commission.

Mandatory minimum sentences have existed at various times in U.S. history, but the current laws FAMM is fighting were mostly enacted in a 1986 anti-drug bill. Members of Congress believed that stiff penalties would deter people from engaging in illegal drug activity and would incapacitate for long periods those who sold drugs. Many of these penalties are mandatory—that is, judges may not impose a penalty less than the number of years chosen by Congress. The most common mandatory sentences are for five and 10 years, and are based on the weight of the drug or the presence of a firearm. These laws prevent judges from considering other relevant factors, such as the defendant's role in the offense or likelihood of committing a future offense.

The sentencing guideline system started in 1987. Congress established the sentencing commission and directed it to write guidelines to combat unjustified sentencing disparity from judge to judge across the country. The guidelines require the sentencing judge to consider various facts about the crime and the defendant. Consideration of these facts leads to a "guideline range," for example: 18 to 24 months. While judges must generally impose a sentence within the range, they have discretion to choose a sentence anywhere within the range, and in unusual cases they may choose a sentence above or below the range if they explain their reasons for doing so.

Mandatory minimum sentencing laws and sentencing guidelines are both ways to limit judicial discretion, but the guidelines are clearly preferable. Unlike blunt mandatory minimums which take account of only the quantity of drugs sold, guidelines permit a judge to consider many relevant facts. Also, the mandatory minimums are "one-size-fits-all," while the guidelines allow for upward or downward departures in unusual cases. Unfortunately, the mandatory sentencing laws supersede or "trump" the sentencing guidelines. At sentencing, judges must determine if the defendant was convicted of a quantity of drugs that triggers a mandatory minimum penalty and if so, impose that sentence regardless of the sentencing guidelines.

There are only two ways to avoid a mandatory minimum sentence. First, the defendant may provide "substantial assistance" to the government by turning in other defendants. Second, some defendants qualify for the "safety valve" that Congress passed in 1994 to address (at FAMM's urging) the excessive sentences served by non-violent drug offenders. If the judge finds the defendant is a low-level, non-violent, first-time offender who qualifies for the safety valve, the defendant may be sentenced under the sentencing guidelines instead of the mandatory minimum sentence law. Although the safety valve is a step in the right direction, the criteria for eligibility is very narrow so thousands of non-violent drug defendants are still sent to prison for decades under mandatory minimum sentencing laws.

State Sentences

The federal government is not the only villain in sentencing policy. Most states also have mandatory sentencing laws.

State mandatory sentencing laws carry the same onerous characteristic of federal laws: they send offenders to prison for defined periods of time without considering all the facts of a case. Like federal laws, drug type and weight usually determine the sentence. In addition, many states have set automatic prison terms for those who sell drugs within 1,000 feet of a school.

Michigan and New York have some of the toughest penalties in the nation. Though in 1998, Michigan rolled back the infamous "650-lifer law" which mandated life in prison without parole for offenders convicted of intent to deliver 650 grams or more of heroin or cocaine, Michigan still retains mandatory sentences of 10, 20, or more years for low-level drug sales and a consecutive sentencing law that allows charges to be "stacked" against an offender. New York's Rockefeller drug laws require automatic 15-years to life sentences for some first-time drug offenders. Efforts are underway in both states to reform these laws.

Prison costs and crowding are forcing some states to reconsider mandatory drug sentencing. Louisiana has dropped mandatory sentencing for a wide variety of non-violent offenses, including drugs. Indiana eliminated mandatory 20-year sentences for cocaine sales. Connecticut granted judges limited discretion in sentencing non-violent drug offenders.

Prosecutors retain a number of options that can affect whether a sentence is tried in a state or federal court. When federal drug laws mandate longer sentences than state laws, prosecutors often opt for federal prosecution.

Not all state mandatory laws deal with drugs. Project Exile adds mandatory sentences to felons possessing a gun, those convicted of possessing both guns and drugs, and those brandishing or using a gun on school grounds.

Six Major Problems

1. Judges can't consider the facts of each case.

In federal and state cases where factors trigger mandatory sentencing laws, a judge must impose at least the mandatory sentence. The judge cannot consider the facts of each case and must disregard such factors as a person's role in the offense or likelihood of rehabilitation. Prior convictions can significantly increase the mandatory sentence. Federal mandatory sentences are doubled for certain repeat offenders. Gun possession, even if not used in a crime, mandates automatic sentences for people with previous felony convictions. In many states, habitual offender laws, like California's "three-strikes law," force judges to send non-violent criminals and drug addicts to prison for decades even if cheaper and more effective options like substance abuse treatment are needed. . . .

2. The type and weight of a drug primarily determines sentence length.

Mandatory minimum drug penalties are based primarily on the type of drug and its weight. When members of Congress enacted mandatory sentencing laws in 1986, they identified specific drugs that would carry minimum prison penalties. For each of those drugs they established a quantity, or weight, that would trigger the five-year and 10-year mandatory prison sentences. . . .

3. They remove checks and balances.

In the absence of judicial discretion, control over sentencing shifts to prosecutors who decide whether an offender gets charged in a way to trigger a mandatory sentence, whether the case goes to state or federal court, and whether the defendant has provided enough information, i.e., cooperation or "substantial assistance" to warrant a reduced sentence. Law enforcement techniques may also have an impact on sentence length. When an undercover agent sets up an offender, that agent may manipulate the transaction to increase the amount of drugs involved and/or the number of transactions. Such manipulation in turn can expose defendants to multiple charges and longer sentences. In some states, defendants must serve each mandatory sentence consecutively. When a prosecutor brings multiple charges, the result can be decades in prison. . . .

Federal Mandatory Drug Sentences (for first offenders)

Type of drug	5-year sentence*	10-year sentence*
LSD	1 gram**	10 grams
Marijuana	100 plants or 100 kilos***	1,000 plants or 1,000 kilos
Crack cocaine	5 grams	50 grams
Powder cocaine	500 grams	5 kilos
Heroin	100 grams	1 kilo
Methamphetamine	5 grams	50 grams
PCP	10 grams	100 grams

* There is no parole in the federal system.
** A gram is roughly equal to a single packet of sweetener.
*** A kilo is equal to 2.2 lb.

Families Against Mandatory Minimums, *Primer on Mandatory Sentences*, no date.

4. They encourage and reward those who inform on others.

As the only way to lower a mandatory sentence, offenders are encouraged to trade information for freedom. Federal and state laws reward those willing to provide prosecutors with "substantial assistance" that divulges the names of persons involved in the crime and details about the crime. This system encourages offenders to lie about others in order to avoid lengthy sentences. Those with a minimal role usually have little or no information to offer and end up serving the mandated sentence. . . .

5. Conspiracy laws make those at the top of the drug trade and low-level offenders equally culpable.

Conspiracy is an agreement between two or more persons to work together to commit an unlawful or criminal act. A conspiracy may be ongoing. Participants may drop out, and others join in. The members do not need to know each other or the part others play, and they do not need to know all the details of the plan or operation. They know, however, the purpose of the conspiracy and agree to participate in it. The agreement need not be formal; participation in itself constitutes agreement. Once found guilty of a drug conspiracy, a defendant can be sentenced based solely on a quantity of drugs distributed by other conspirators so long as she played some role, for example, as a lookout, order taker, or go-between. The law requires that before she can be sentenced based on those other amounts, however, those amounts must have been both "reasonably foreseeable" to her and "within the scope of her agreement." Sentencing rules about foreseeability and scope set real limits on the broad reach of conspiracy law. Because those rules are complex and can be difficult to apply, mistakes are made—mistakes that can mean even longer sentences than the defendant otherwise would have received. For example, even low-level participants—those who may have distributed only a small amount of drugs or been only tangentially involved (for example, through a girlfriend or boyfriend)—have been known to receive sentences mistakenly based on all the drugs distributed by members of the conspiracy, even amounts distributed before they agreed to join the conspiracy. In addition, in many states, drug defendants are routinely charged and sentenced separately with delivery and with conspiracy to deliver, thus potentially (sometimes) doubling mandatory sentences for the same quantity of drugs. . . .

6. Low-level offenders often get longer sentences than high-level dealers.

Congress established mandatory sentences with the intention of locking up high-level drug traffickers. But only 11 percent of those incarcerated in federal prisons on drug charges fit that definition, according to the U.S. Sentencing Commission. The rest are low-level offenders. A provision of the law allows offenders to receive lesser sentences by providing "substantial assistance" with the case, either by setting up others or telling on others. Such cooperation is the only way offenders can reduce mandatory sentences. Unfortunately, high-level traffickers, who know the workings of a drug organization, have much information to share, but low-level participants have little or no knowledge of value. The result? Low-level defendants frequently serve longer sentences than those at the top of the drug trade. . . .

FAMM's Goals

Restore judicial discretion so the punishment fits the crime. Judges—not lawmakers, prosecutors, or law enforcement officers—should determine appropriate sentences. Their training, experience and neutrality place judges in the best position to weigh the many factors that should affect a sentence.

Replace mandatory sentencing laws with flexible sentencing guidelines. Federal and many state sentencing guideline systems provide judges with a range of sentences for offenses. Guidelines allow judges to consider all facts of the case, yet prevent wildly disparate sentences for similar offenses.

Strengthen and expand prevention and treatment programs to provide more cost-effective punishments. A 1997 RAND study found that treatment of heavy drug users was eight-to-nine times more cost-effective than long (six to seven-year) mandatory sentences in reducing drug use, sales and drug-related crime.

6

VIEWPOINT

"[Mandatory minimum sentencing] provides prosecutors with a valuable weapon in the fight against major drug traffickers."

Mandatory Minimum Sentences Are Effective in the War Against Drugs

John Roth

John Roth is the chief of the Narcotic and Dangerous Drug Section of the Department of Justice, Criminal Division. The following viewpoint is his testimony before a congressional committee on drug policy. Roth argues that mandatory minimum sentences are a valuable tool in the war on drugs. Mandatory minimums ensure that criminals convicted of similar crimes receive similar sentences, thus protecting public safety. He adds that the guidelines for mandatory minimum sentences offer a "safety valve" that reduces the sentence for low-level drug criminals who help investigators gather evidence against the higher-level offenders. As a result, Roth asserts, sentences for drug crimes are more uniform and fair.

As you read, consider the following questions:

1. What law enforcement interests are advanced by mandatory minimum sentencing, according to Roth?
2. Which specific offenders is the safety valve provision directed toward, as cited by the author?
3. How does Roth counter the claim that mandatory minimums put too much discretion in the hands of the prosecutor?

John Roth, testimony before the Subcommittee on Criminal Justice, Drug Policy, and Human Resources Committee on Government Reform Review of Drug Sentencing Policies, Guidelines, and Practices, May 11, 2000.

As the Nation's prosecutor, the Department of Justice enforces federal criminal laws enacted by Congress, including those laws that carry mandatory minimum sentences. We believe that the existing sentencing scheme for serious federal drug offenses provides prosecutors with a valuable weapon in the fight against major drug traffickers. At the same time, the current mandatory minimum laws strike the right balance by allowing nonviolent offenders without significant criminal histories an opportunity to be sentenced without regard to the mandatory minimums.

In narcotics enforcement, mandatory minimum sentences are reserved principally for serious drug offenders, based on the quantity of narcotics distributed, and for related firearms violators. Criminals with prior drug felony convictions or who have operated a continuing criminal enterprise also receive stricter sentences.

Mandatory Minimums Help Law Enforcement

These crimes threaten our national safety and must be prosecuted vigorously. Mandatory minimums assist in the effective prosecution of drug offenses by advancing several important law enforcement interests.

First, mandatory minimums increase the certainty and predictability of incarceration for certain crimes, assuring uniform sentencing for similarly situated offenders. The Department believes that uniform and predictable sentences deter certain types of criminal behavior by forewarning the potential offender that, if apprehended and convicted, his punishment will be certain and substantial. Mandatory minimum sentences also incapacitate serious dangerous offenders for substantial periods of time, thereby enhancing public safety.

In addition to serving important sentencing goals, mandatory minimum sentences also provide an indispensable tool for prosecutors, because the law provides relief from mandatory sentences if a defendant provides substantial assistance in the investigation or prosecution of another person who has committed an offense. This assistance can take the form of truthful and complete testimony against other traffickers. Unlike bank robbery, where the witnesses might be ordinary citizens, in narcotics violations the only witnesses typically are other criminals. Drug dealers take pains to ensure that their distribution takes place far from the prying eyes of law enforcement, and the more sophisticated the drug dealer, the more cautious he is about dealing with anyone who might be a law enforcement officer.

As a result, Congress has given us a powerful tool to conduct effective narcotics investigations. The offer of relief from a mandatory minimum sentence in exchange for truthful testimony and other forms of substantial assistance allows us to move up the chain of the drug supply, offering incentives against the lesser dealers in exchange for substantial assistance against the leaders. Substantial assistance agreements give us the best evidence we have concerning a trafficking organization—the sworn truthful testimony or other assistance of someone on the inside of the organization. It allows us to strip away the secrecy in which narcotics traffickers conduct their business and to obtain the truth.

Such cooperation is essential in our efforts to combat local, national, and international drug trafficking and related crimes. Federal prosecutors use substantial assistance departures every day to prove their cases against significant traffickers, and it is no exaggeration to say that their job would be nearly impossible without it. Courts have time and again approved the use of these departures as a legitimate tool in the enforcement of federal criminal law.

The Safety Valve Provision

While the Department views mandatory minimums as an effective law enforcement tool, we also recognize the need to apply the provisions appropriately, protecting the rights of the individual defendant and avoiding miscarriages of justice. In this regard, the law and policy governing mandatory minimums has continually evolved. Primary among these changes has been, in 1994, the addition of the so-called "safety valve provision," located at section 3553(f) of Title 18, United States Code, which directs courts to impose a sentence "without regard to any statutory minimum sentence" in certain cases. Specifically, the safety valve allows even an otherwise serious drug defendant who did not use a firearm or violence, was not a leader or manager, and who does not have a serious criminal history, to be sentenced below the statutory mandatory minimum sentence, provided the offense did not result in death or serious bodily injury. The defendant, in exchange, must truthfully tell the government all of the facts known to him about his crime and related conduct. The sentencing guidelines also provide a reduction in the guideline sentence for safety-valve defendants.

A Prosecutor's Most Important Tool

Most front-line federal prosecutors including those who deal with narcotics and organized crime cases strongly support tough mandatory minimum sentences for drug trafficking. . . .

Minimum sentences are perhaps the single most important law enforcement tool available to prosecutors in targeting and successfully convicting high-level drug dealers. Moreover, the minimums are not absolute: Low-level defendants can avoid them by cooperating with prosecutors.

Jay Apperson, *Washington Post*, February 27, 1994.

Let me give you an example of how the safety valve works. A defendant is charged with the possession with intent to distribute five kilograms of cocaine, which has a wholesale price of approximately $100,000. He does not have a significant criminal history, did not possess a firearm or otherwise use violence, and has expressed an acceptance of responsibility for his crime. Ordinarily, he would be subject to a mandatory minimum sentence of 10 years. However, because he is eligible for the safety valve, he would be subject to a sentencing range of 70 to 87 months, or a little under six years on the low end of the range. [Sentencing level 32 minus 3 (acceptance of responsibility) minus 2 (safety valve) = level 27.] If the court found that he had played a minor role in the offense, he would be sentenced within a range of 57 to 71 months, or a little under five years on the low end of the range. [Level 32 minus 3 (acceptance of responsibility) minus 2 (safety valve) minus 2 (minor role).]

The safety valve provision has succeeded in its purpose of preventing the mandatory minimum drug provisions from sweeping too broadly. Its provisions are mandatory, not discretionary, and it is widely used. According to the Sentencing Commission data for Fiscal Year 1998, there were 12,055 drug defendants sentenced in which a mandatory minimum was applicable. Of those cases, 4,185, or approximately one third, were provided relief from a mandatory minimum sentence. These statistics demonstrate that the safety valve provisions are being applied regularly by federal judges, allowing greater flexibility in sentencing while maintaining appropriately serious penalties for the serious drug traffickers who use violence, who lead others in criminal activity, or who have significant criminal histories.

As a result, in large part, of these legislative amendments to the mandatory minimum sentencing provisions, sentences for federal drug cases on the whole have decreased. In 1992, the average drug sentence was 89 months; in 1998, the average drug sentence was 78 months, a 12 percent decline.

Uniform and Equitable

We have an obligation to apply the law fairly and without discrimination. The Department of Justice promotes uniform and equitable application of the sentencing guidelines and the mandatory minimum sentences by requiring prosecutors to charge the most serious, readily provable offense or offenses consistent with the defendant's conduct. Similarly, prosecutors must seek a plea to the most serious readily provable offense charged. While these rules are subject to limited exceptions, the prosecutor must have the specific approval of the United States Attorney or designated supervisory level official, and the rationale for diverging from the basic rule must be explicitly set forth in the prosecutor's file.

The Prosecutor's Role

Finally, I would like to address the contention that the mandatory minimums put too much discretion in the hands of the prosecutor. First, it is important to note that the provisions of the "safety valve" are mandatory, not discretionary. As a result, if a criminal defendant meets the factors set forth in the statute, then there is no discretion on the part of either the prosecutor or the court. The defendant will be sentenced without regard to the mandatory minimum sentence. Secondly, if the prosecutor makes a substantial assistance motion to the court because the defendant has assisted in the prosecution of another, the court has complete discretion to sentence the defendant without regard to the sentencing guideline range. While the prosecutor can recommend a sentence, the court is not bound by that recommendation and may sentence the defendant to whatever the court deems is appropriate. Finally, because the sentencing guidelines are based to a great extent on offense conduct, rather than simply on the crime charged, there are significant limitations on the prosecutor's ability to determine the guideline sentence by the charges he or she files, particularly with respect to sentencing in drug-trafficking cases.

Taken as a whole, the Department of Justice believes that the system of mandatory minimums is fair and effective, promoting the interests of public safety while protecting the rights of individuals. We also recognize the need periodically to review the mandatory minimum provisions and adjust their levels in light of experience.

Periodical Bibliography

The following articles have been selected to supplement the diverse views presented in this chapter.

Norm R. Allen Jr. — "Reforming the Incarceration Nation," *Free Inquiry*, July 2001.

Jennifer Bleyer — "Prison Converts," *Progressive*, June 2001.

Philip C. Chronakis — "The Bravery of Being Out of Range: N.J.'s Failed Drug-Sentencing Laws," *New Jersey Law Journal*, July 8, 2002.

Shirley Dicks — "A Mother's View of the Death Penalty," *Free Inquiry*, July 2001.

Catherine Edwards — "Restorative Justice," *Insight on the News*, July 26, 1999.

Wendy Kaminer — "Games Prosecutors Play," *American Prospect*, September 1999.

Donna Lyons — "Conviction for Addiction," *State Legislatures*, June 2002.

Cait Murphy — "Think that Stuffing Prisons with Lawbreakers Makes Sense?" *Fortune*, April 30, 2001.

Richard A. Posner — "Capital Crimes," *New Republic*, April 1, 2002.

Margot Roosevelt — "Bizarre, Draconian, and Disproportionate?" *Time*, November 11, 2002.

Duane Ruth-Heffelbower — "Restorative Justice: Making Things Right," *Witness*, November 1998.

Wilson A. Schooley — "Is Price No Object in Our Bid to Make Crime Never Pay?" *Human Rights*, April 2002.

Richard Taylor — "Getting Tough on Crime: What Does It Mean?" *Free Inquiry*, July 2001.

Stuart Taylor Jr. — "It's Time to Stop Packing Prisons with Two-Bit Crack Users," *National Journal*, May 4, 2002.

William Vance Trollinger Jr. — "In Lockdown America," *Christian Century*, June 20, 2001.

Michael Vitiello — "Three Strikes Laws," *Human Rights*, April 2002.

Julia Vitull-Martin — "The Jury's Still Out," *Commonweal*, August 16, 2002.

Chapter 4

What Rights Should Be a Part of the Criminal Justice System?

Chapter Preface

The *Miranda* ruling requires police to warn suspects that they have the right to remain silent when questioned by police; that any statements they make to police can be used during their trial; that they have the right to have an attorney present during questioning; and that if they cannot afford a lawyer, one will be provided for them. *Miranda* has become such a part of the American criminal justice system that many were surprised when the U.S. Supreme Court decided to review the decision in 2000. At issue was a law, known as Section 3501, that Congress had passed in 1968 in an attempt to nullify the court's 1966 decision in *Miranda v. Arizona*. The law provides that the *Miranda* warning is not necessary if it can be shown that a suspect's confession was given voluntarily.

In the 2000 case, *Dickerson v. United States*, Charles Dickerson confessed to robbing seven banks in Maryland, but then appealed his conviction, claiming he had not been read his rights prior to his confession. Conservative lawyers urged the appeals court to uphold his conviction based on Section 3501. The appeals court decreed that Section 3501 overturned the Supreme Court's decision in *Miranda*, essentially ruling that police were no longer required to tell suspects their rights.

The Supreme Court overturned the appeals court ruling and reaffirmed its original 1966 *Miranda* ruling in *Dickerson*. According to Chief Justice William Rehnquist, who authored the decision, "We hold that *Miranda*, being a constitutional decision of this Court, may not be in effect overruled by an Act of Congress, and we decline to overrule *Miranda* ourselves. We therefore hold that *Miranda* and its progeny in this Court govern the admissibility of statements made during custodial interrogation in both state and federal courts."

The authors in the following chapter debate whether the original *Miranda* ruling should be overturned as well as whether other controversial defendants' rights are protected by the Constitution.

VIEWPOINT 1

"Victims of violent crime have important rights that deserve protection in our Constitution."

A Victims' Rights Constitutional Amendment Is Necessary

George W. Bush

George W. Bush is the forty-third president of the United States. In the following viewpoint, Bush argues that the rights of criminals are duly protected by the U.S. Constitution, and the rights of their victims should also be protected. He asserts that few crime victims are kept informed about the status of the criminal proceedings; by ignoring them, the criminal justice systems victimizes them a second time. He concludes that a victims' rights amendment would give crime victims a sense of justice and allow them to have more active participation in their cases.

As you read, consider the following questions:

1. How does Bush describe the needs of crime victims in the criminal justice system?
2. What happened thirty years ago to help crime victims, according to the author?
3. What are the basic pledges to American crime victims contained in the amendment, as cited by Bush?

George W. Bush, "President Calls for Crime Victims' Rights Amendment," www.whitehouse.gov, April 16, 2002.

Justice is one of the defining commitments of America. In our war against terror, I constantly remind our fellow citizens we seek justice, not revenge. We seek justice for victims. We seek justice for their families. And for justice to prevail in our struggle for freedom, we must rout out terrorist threats wherever they exist. And that's exactly what this country is going to do. And while the war goes on, and while our fight for freedom continues, we will continue to work for justice at home, including justice for the victims of violent crime. . . .

Protecting the Victims

As Attorney General John Ashcroft mentioned, in the year 2000, Americans were victims of millions of crimes. Behind each of these numbers is a terrible trauma, a story of suffering and a story of lost security. Yet the needs of victims are often an afterthought in our criminal justice system. It's not just, it's not fair, and it must change. As we protect the rights of criminals, we must take equal care to protect the rights of the victims.

Many of the victims of crime have gotten a crash course in the complications and frustrations of our criminal justice system. One victim put it this way: "They explained the defendant's constitutional right to the nth degree. They couldn't do this and they couldn't do that because of his constitutional rights. And I wondered what mine were. And they told me, I hadn't got any.". . .

But too often, our system fails to inform victims about proceedings involving bail and pleas and sentencing and even about the trials themselves. Too often, the process fails to take the safety of victims into account when deciding whether to release dangerous offenders.

Too often, the financial losses of victims are ignored. And too often, victims are not allowed to address the court at sentencing and explain their suffering, or even to be present in the courtroom where their victimizers are being tried.

When our criminal justice systems treats victims as irrelevant bystanders, they are victimized for a second time. And because Americans are justifiably proud of our system and expect it to treat us fairly, the second violation of our rights can be traumatic. "It's like a huge slap," said one victim, "because you think the system will protect you. It's maddening and frightening."

A Grass-Roots Movement

Thirty years ago, a grass-roots movement began to stand up for the rights of victims. It resulted in domestic violence shelters, support groups for families of homicide victims, rape crisis centers. They exist in cities and neighborhoods all across America, because Americans care about their neighbors in need.

One good example is in John's home state of Missouri. It's called Aids—Aid for Victims of Crime, Inc., in which volunteers provide counseling and court advocacy and other essential services to the victims of crime. Victims' rights groups are active every single day. There isn't a day that goes by that they're not involved in somebody's life, and they're especially important during times of disaster and crisis.

You know, when the bomber hit Oklahoma City in 1995, victims' rights groups were on the scene immediately thereafter to help. And the same happened after 9/11 [2001] in New York, Washington, [and] Pennsylvania. Victims' rights groups were there, hundreds of counselors and chaplains and social workers, victims' service providers helped their fellow Americans deal with the unspeakable pain and suffering caused by the terrorist murders.

The Attorney General will shortly present awards to outstanding individuals and groups for their work on behalf of victims. I had the honor of meeting the winners, and I want to congratulate them publicly for loving your neighbor just like you'd like to be loved yourself. You've chosen to live out the words of Saint Paul: "Be not overcome of evil, but overcome evil with good."

As our nation struggles to overcome the evil of September the 11th, your lives, the example you set, stand out as models of compassion and integrity.

The Nation Begins to Respond

The victims' rights movement has touched the conscience of this country, and our criminal justice system has begun to respond, treating victims with greater respect. The states, as well as the federal government, have passed legal protections for victims. However, those laws are insufficient to fully recognize the rights of crime victims.

State Laws Are Not Enough

Why aren't amendments to state constitutions adequate to satisfy the needs of victims and their families? Just ask Bob Preston, a leading Florida advocate of the constitutional amendment. Preston helped pass a state law giving victims the right to speak at parole hearings. Yet, even after its enactment, the man convicted of murdering Preston's daughter, Wendy, had a parole hearing—and no one told Wendy's family. Preston was incensed. Roberta Roper, another leader of the victims-rights movement, was barred from observing the Maryland trial of the men who kidnapped, raped and murdered her daughter Stephanie. The reason was a rule that says no witnesses may observe the testimony of any other witness lest they untruthfully tailor their testimony to match the other's. And yet, the sole subject of Roper's testimony was the undisputed ownership of the car Stephanie had been driving. Roper was devastated.

Roper later learned the same rule was followed so slavishly that it was a common tactic of defense attorneys to list as potential witnesses the family members of murder victims so as to keep them out of the most important public proceedings of their lives—and then never to call them to the stand.

The indignities crime victims face in the justice system are a plain violation of human rights. There is something in the American expression "I want my day in court" that speaks to a universal impulse to seek societal redress of wrongs in formal settings in which the person wronged may observe and participate. Indeed, except for the English-speaking countries, virtually all of the justice systems of the West make victims an actual or virtual party to the prosecution.

Marlene A. Young, *Insight*, August 31, 1998.

Victims of violent crime have important rights that deserve protection in our Constitution. And so today, I announce my support for the bipartisan Crime Victims' Rights amendment to the Constitution of the United States.

This amendment is sponsored by Senator [Diane] Feinstein of California, Senator [Jon] Kyl of Arizona—one a Democrat, one a Republican. Both great Americans.

This amendment makes some basic pledges to Americans. Victims of violent crime deserve the right to be notified of public proceedings involving the crime. They deserve to be heard at public proceedings regarding the criminal's sentence or potential release. They deserve to have their safety considered. They deserve consideration of their claims of restitution. We must guarantee these rights for all the victims of violent crime in America.

The Feinstein-Kyl Amendment was written with care, and strikes a proper balance. Our legal system properly protects the rights of the accused in the Constitution. But it does not provide similar protection for the rights of victims, and that must change.

The protection of victims' rights is one of those rare instances when amending the Constitution is the right thing to do. And the Feinstein-Kyl Crime Victims' Rights Amendment is the right way to do it.

May God bless you all, and may God bless America.

VIEWPOINT 2

"It is unclear . . . just how those [victims'] rights would operate, just how they are invoked, and how remedies for their violation would work."

A Victims' Rights Constitutional Amendment Is Unnecessary

Roger Pilon

In the following viewpoint, Roger Pilon argues that a constitutional amendment to protect the rights of crime victims is unnecessary. Many state and local governments have passed laws to help crime victims, and they are able to do so more quickly and better than a constitutional amendment could. Furthermore, Pilon contends that sometimes the government's interests in prosecuting a criminal may conflict with the victim's interests, and the state's primary role is to protect the rights of the people rather than individual victims. He asserts that victims have their own forum—civil law—in which they can seek redress. Pilon is a senior fellow at the Cato Institute and the director of Cato's Center for Constitutional Studies.

As you read, consider the following questions:

1. How does Pilon describe the rights of defendants as enumerated in the Constitution?
2. How might the interests of the people differ from the interests of the victim, according to the author?
3. How is the victims' rights amendment like a legacy in a pauper's will, in Pilon's opinion?

Roger Pilon, statement before the Committee on the Judiciary, United States Senate, April 28, 1998.

Although I am opposed to amending the Constitution for the purpose of protecting the rights of crime victims, I want to make it very clear at the outset that I fully support the basic aims of this proposal. Too often when a prosecutor takes over the prosecution of a crime, the victim is all but forgotten. We need to do more than we sometimes do to help the victims of crime. At the same time, for both constitutional and practical reasons, this amendment is not the best way to accomplish that end.

A Serious Matter

Amending the Constitution is a serious matter. Clearly, the provisions of Article V that enable us to do so were put there to be used. But just as clearly, experience has taught us that those provisions are to be used only when circumstances plainly warrant it. When other, more flexible means are available to accomplish the same ends—especially when we may need to refine what we do in light of experience—prudence alone suggests that we employ such means, that we not lock ourselves inflexibly in our basic law, the Constitution.

On the subject at hand, federal, state, and local governments are already moving, and have been for some time, to better provide for the victims of crime. Through ordinary legislation or state constitutions they are achieving every aim of this proposal more quickly and with equal effect and greater flexibility. Thus, there is no compelling reason to pursue such ends by amending our basic charter of government.

But if there is no compelling reason to amend the Constitution to provide for victims' rights, there are compelling reasons for not amending the Constitution for that end. . . .

As a structural matter, such rights as are found in our Constitution, either enumerated or unenumerated, are invoked ordinarily when some governmental action either proceeds without authority or in violation of a recognized right (e.g., any authorized action that implicates rights of speech or religion). Thus, the putative authority of the government is pitted against the putative right of the individual or organization (to be free from such action, or from such an application of an otherwise authorized action).

Here, however, we have a three-way relationship, which

raises havoc with our traditional adversarial system. How, for example, do we resolve the potential conflicts among the authority of the state to prosecute, the right of the accused to a speedy but fair trial, and the right of the victim to "a final disposition of the proceedings relating to the crime free from unreasonable delay"? If judicial "balancing" poses serious jurisprudential problems in our adversarial system today—and it does—then those problems will only be exacerbated under this amendment.

In the larger context, then, the rights of defendants that we find in the Constitution make perfectly good sense. They are restraints on government power. The federal government may pursue the ends it is authorized to pursue, but it must respect our rights in the process. The government may enact and enforce customs laws, for example, but it may not engage in warrantless searches of our homes or businesses in the process. And if it prosecutes us in the course of enforcing those laws, it must respect the rights of defendants as set forth in the Constitution and the Bill of Rights.

Thus, given the basic defensive way we constituted ourselves, it is not surprising that the rights of crime victims are not mentioned in the Constitution. That does not mean that there are no such rights, however, for the Seventh Amendment incorporated the common law into our constitutional order, by reference, and the right of victims to bring actions against those who victimize them is at the core of the common law. We must not forget, therefore, that the *primary* way in which victims have their rights vindicated is not through the criminal but through the civil law. It is the business of the state to protect us from each other, as much as it can, and to punish those who injure us. It is our business to seek redress from those who injure us, to vindicate the rights that have been violated by the criminal.

A Conflict of Interest

That vindication may be achieved in part through the criminal proceeding, to be sure, for most victims have an interest and even a right in seeing the criminal get his comeuppance. But the proceeding belongs primarily to "the people," whose interests and rights may be identical to those of the victim, but may also be at variance with those of the victim. Sometimes the prosecutor will want to put the criminal away, for example, but other times he may want to strike a deal with the criminal in order to reach other, more dangerous criminals, criminals that are of no concern to the victim, who wants this particular perpetrator punished. In such cases, the crucial question is, whose forum is it? Under our system, where we delegated law enforcement for the most part to the state, it is the people's forum, with the prosecutor representing the interests of the people.

Asay. © 1998 by *The Gazette*. Reprinted by permission of the Creators Syndicate.

It is crucial, therefore, that there be two forums—criminal and civil—for there are two sets of interests to be pursued, and they are not always in harmony. It is for that reason, however, that it is crucial also to recognize that an uncritical concern for "victims' rights" may very well muddy the water. More precisely, when rights that belong properly in the civil forum are transported to the criminal forum, confusion and conflict may ensue. That is a very real risk with this proposal.

Consider, for example, the victim's right "to an order of restitution from the convicted offender," as set forth in Section 1 of the proposed constitutional amendment. Perhaps such details as would constitute a restitution order could be incorporated into the prosecutor's case against the defendant, aimed at determining his guilt or innocence, but that kind of concern rests properly with the victim, not with the people or their representative, the prosecutor. When representing separate parties, there is always the potential for conflict of interest, of course. That is clear here. The victim's interest in restitution may vitiate punishment. The people's interest in punishment may vitiate restitution. Which interest should prevail under this amendment? And would the failure to convict—perhaps because of the higher standard of proof for a criminal conviction—undermine any right of the victim to a restitution order—which might have been obtained in a civil action against the defendant?

Other Problems

Thus, when we cloud the theory of our system of justice with an amendment of this kind, we give rise to all manner of practical problems. Most generally, those problems surround the very nature of the victim's claims. In the proposed amendment they are called "rights," but it is unclear to me, at least, just how those rights would operate, just how they are invoked, and how remedies for their violation would work. In determining any release from custody, for example, the victim would have a "right" to "consideration" for his safety. That "right" is either so vague as to be all but meaningless, or it is not. If not, then what does it mean? Do not most prosecutors now take such "consideration" into their calculations? How would things change under this amendment? Most importantly, would the victim have a claim against a prosecutor who was insufficiently considerate? Section 2 of the proposed amendment grants the victim standing to "assert" the rights established by the amendment—whatever that means. But the rest of Section 2 takes everything back, suggesting that the victim has no real "rights" after all.

There is, in short, a disturbing air of "aspiration" about

this proposal. Like the generous legacy in a pauper's will, it promises much but delivers little. Clearly, rights without remedies are worse than useless: they are empty promises that in time undermine confidence in the very document that contains them—the United States Constitution, in this case. But a remedy is ordinarily realized through litigation. Before this amendment goes any further, therefore, it is incumbent upon those who support it to show how victims will or might litigate to realize their rights, and what their doing so implies for other rights in our constitutional system. I can imagine several scenarios under this amendment, none of which is clear, all of which—by virtue of being constitutionalized—will make the plight of victims not better but worse. We owe more than empty promises to those for whom the system has already failed once.

3

VIEWPOINT

"The Miranda *ruling . . . unreasonably handcuffs law enforcement where the danger to civil liberties is marginal; it thus should be abandoned."*

The *Miranda* Warning Impedes Law Enforcement

Bruce Fein

In 1966 the U.S. Supreme Court ruled in *Miranda v. Arizona* that police officers must inform all arrested suspects of their rights prior to questioning. Bruce Fein argues in the following viewpoint that if the suspect voluntarily offers a confession to the police before the *Miranda* warning is given, the confession should be admissible in court. Prohibiting the admission of the confession during the trial thwarts justice, he contends, and has a minimal impact on a suspect's civil liberties. Fein, a former associate deputy U.S. attorney, is now in private practice specializing in constitutional law.

As you read, consider the following questions:

1. What evidence does Fein present to support his contention that abolishing the *Miranda* warning will not lead to coerced confessions?
2. According to the author, which law enforcement agency has indicated it will continue to issue *Miranda* rulings regardless of the Supreme Court ruling on the case?
3. Why are voluntary confessions, given without the knowledge of *Miranda*'s rights, highly moral and laudatory, in Fein's opinion?

Bruce Fein, "Q: Should the High Court Let Police Avoid Giving the *Miranda* Warning? Yes: *Miranda* Handcuffs Police Even When the Danger to Civil Liberties Is Marginal," *Insight on the News*, May 15, 2000.

Editor's Note: In June 2000, the U.S. Supreme Court upheld the constitutionality of the Miranda *ruling in the case of* Dickerson v. United States.

Let's put aside the customary polemics and sloganeering that surround *Miranda vs. Arizona* (1966), a U.S. Supreme Court decree generally excluding the use of voluntary confessions in criminal prosecutions if elicited during police custodial interrogation without first alerting the suspect of his right to refuse cooperation and to the assistance of an attorney.

Rarely does a suspect altruistically or otherwise confess to crimes committed by others reminiscent of Sidney Carton in *A Tale of Two Cities.* And in the event of that *rara avis*, the suspect during the criminal trial may attack the reliability of his voluntary confession by explaining his motivation to lie.

The Fifth Amendment privilege against compulsory self-incrimination testifies to the nation's abhorrence of forcing a defendant to convict himself instead of saddling the government with the burden of gathering incriminating evidence, even if the result means that some guilty persons go free. That same constitutional tilt in favor of individual liberty also is found in the requirement of proof beyond a reasonable doubt and jury unanimity to obtain a conviction. In sum, the Constitution generally celebrates the creed that it is better that no innocent be wrongfully convicted than that all the guilty be imprisoned.

The *Miranda* ruling, however, unreasonably handcuffs law enforcement where the danger to civil liberties is marginal; it thus should be abandoned as a Fifth Amendment edict binding on every police officer in the country.

Take the following hypothetical example. The police arrest a murder suspect and return to headquarters for a videotaped interrogation. Refreshments are provided, and a police inspector with the shrewdness of Sherlock Holmes elicits a confession by playing on the suspect's emotional vulnerabilities. Attempts to gather incriminating evidence through search warrants and witnesses prove futile. At trial, the videotape is authenticated and categorically discredits any claim of police coercion. The confession would be excluded under *Miranda* and the prosecution foiled, however, because the suspect was not previously informed of his right not to cooperate and to the presence and assistance of a lawyer.

That makes no sense. The murderer escapes punishment—and is likely to commit mayhem again because of appalling rates of recidivism—yet the police did nothing troubling to civil liberties. Proponents of *Miranda* might argue that my hypothetical is uncommon, that proof of guilt beyond a reasonable doubt can be assembled in ordinary cases without confessions, that videotaped interrogations are unusual and that police are inclined to lie under oath about the circumstances of confessions to establish their voluntariness. Ernesto Miranda himself, the criminal star of the *Miranda* precedent, was convicted on retrial despite the suppression of his confession.

The Costs of *Miranda*

These arguments hold force but are unconvincing. Meticulous empirical studies conducted by Paul Cassell, professor of law at the University of Utah, demonstrate that *Miranda* warnings have substantially plunged crime clearance rates by slashing the incidence of voluntary and reliable confessions. Incriminating evidence frequently is unavailable, especially when a conviction is overturned on appeal years after the initial trial when witnesses may have died or disappeared or their memories dimmed. Cassell estimates that more than 130,000 crimes of violence and approximately 300,000 property crimes go unsolved annually because of the silence encouraged by *Miranda*. And who loses from such thwarted law enforcement? Not the rich and famous, but the poor and minorities who predominate among the long list of crime victims.

Furthermore, searching for incriminating evidence despite voluntary and reliable confessions is not without cost. FBI statistics show that only one in five felonies leads to an arrest; in four of five incidents, no one is apprehended. Insofar as *Miranda* compels investigators to prove guilt without confessions, law enforcement is diverted from solving other serious crimes.

Voluntary Confessions

At present, police interrogations and suspect confessions characteristically are neither taped nor recorded. And police lying under oath to a judge to establish that the suspect voluntarily chose to speak when in fact coercion was employed is a risk. But it seems tolerable.

The defendant enjoys a constitutional right to counsel and to testify in his own defense. The police version of the interrogation can thus be challenged by contrary testimony by the accused and by cross-examination of the interrogators by defense counsel. Trial judges, moreover, are not ingenues. A hefty percentage are former prosecutors alert to the likelihood of police prevarications. Judges also are independent and owe no loyalty to the prosecution. In sum, police deceit about the circumstances of interrogation is thus unlikely to escape detection. A 1968 federal statute endorsing voluntariness in federal prosecutions also partly deters police overreaching. The law, whose constitutionality in light of *Miranda* is at issue in the Supreme Court case of *Dickerson v. United States*, directs the judge to consider the following: the time between the defendant's arrest and arraignment, his knowledge of the crime charged, his understanding of his right to silence and to the assistance of counsel and the presence or not of the accused's lawyer when the confession was made. The statute would be improved, nevertheless, by a directive that confessions either be videotaped or recorded unless the circumstances would make such reliable evidence unreasonable or impractical. Also needed is a provision that exposes police interrogators to liability for damages to a suspect in custody for the knowing and malicious resort to unconstitutional coercion to extract a confession.

Detractors of the voluntariness standard insist that its elusiveness will occasion a spiraling of wasteful litigation and slow lead-footed justice to a snail's pace. The *Miranda* rules, in contrast, are clear and easy to apply.

But that defense of *Miranda* over voluntariness is feeble. Its application is fraught with uncertainties only marginally less troublesome. The Supreme Court, for instance, crafted a public-safety exception to *Miranda* in *New York v. Quarles* (1984). Litigation also frequently ensues over whether police interrogation was "custodial," whether the suspect waived his *Miranda* rights or requested the assistance of counsel, whether a *Miranda* violation has tainted derivative evidence and whether police soliloquies calculated to evoke a response from the suspect constitute "interrogation." Indeed, law-school casebooks typically devote more than 100 pages to explicating *Miranda* and its offshoots.

Furthermore, abandoning *Miranda* as a constitutional requirement for every law-enforcement officer in every federal, state and local jurisdiction still would permit its retention as a matter of policy in order to avoid more vexing voluntariness litigation or otherwise. The Department of Justice in *Dickerson*, for example, has informed the Supreme Court that the FBI will continue to provide *Miranda* warnings whether or not the precedent is overruled. Other jurisdictions might chart the same course due to worries about police abuses. And such law-enforcement policy decisions would not be permanent. They always could be altered in light of experience and the changing incidence of crime within the jurisdiction.

Miranda Makes Things More Difficult

The *Miranda* warnings do not make things simpler, as is often claimed. They just give the guilty two bases on which to challenge a confession in the courts rather than one. With *Miranda*, confessed criminals can challenge not only whether they were given Miranda warnings at just the right time and under the proper circumstances, but also—even if they were—whether their confessions were voluntary. This is not a big time-saver. Instead of being on the street fighting crime, cops spend hours in court for suppression hearings.

Moreover, *Miranda* has led to a dramatic drop in criminal confessions, the single most important tool in law enforcement. About one-fifth of suspects are never questioned at all because of *Miranda*, and another 16 percent invoke their rights, ending all questioning.

Ann Coulter, "*Miranda* Means More Criminals Stay on the Streets," www.vexpress.com, January 5, 2000.

Champions of *Miranda* occasionally insist that the law-enforcement exploitation of citizen ignorance of constitutional rights is immoral or unsavory. *Miranda*, it is said, simply informs the ignorant of their rights to frustrate the law through silence and the assistance of a shrewd attorney. The Constitution grants these rights, however, not because confessions inherently are evil but to safeguard against both unreliable verdicts and law-enforcement zealots. Reliable and voluntary confessions stemming from ignorance of rights are highly moral and laudatory even if a seasoned recidivist veteran of police interrogations would have remained silent because they promote accurate jury verdicts and the punishment of the guilty. The voluntariness standard simultaneously ensures against unfair and deplorable police coercion. In sum, few would dispute that on a moral scale it is worse that a criminal circumvent justice than that ignorance of the law lead him voluntarily to confess guilt under police interrogation.

More serious is the criticism that *Miranda* is praiseworthy because it narrows the significant defense discrepancies between rich and poor suspects. To paraphrase Anatole France, the law, in its majestic equality, entitles both the highly educated, wealthy and well-represented and their ill-educated, poor, and destitute counterparts to know about the right to silence and to receive masterful legal advice.

Unprivileged suspects indeed are less likely to know of their constitutional rights and thus more likely to benefit from *Miranda* than the rich and famous, and ignorance is more widespread among racial or ethnic minorities than among whites.

But perfect equality in the legal system is impossible; so with a system of private property and its inevitable wealth differences. Money buys the best defense attorneys, who routinely charge $400 to $500 per hour. And astute lawyers are vastly more talented in discrediting the prosecution's case than are the more typical and affordable mediocrities. The wealthy thus are more advantaged than middle- or lower-income earners in seeking to evade justice. That is regrettable. But the modest remedy *Miranda* provides seems far worse than the disease. It multiplies the thwarting of justice by minorities and the poor in the name of evenhandedness, but the criminal beneficiaries prey mostly on those hapless groups. Isn't protecting them from criminal victimization more worthy than releasing their guilty predators, even at the cost of more wealth-based justice?

4

VIEWPOINT

"Miranda protects law enforcement officials from the suspicion that they coerced a confession from someone in their custody."

The *Miranda* Warning Should Not Be Abolished

Charles Levendosky

Charles Levendosky argues in the following viewpoint that the *Miranda* warning—a statement the police give suspects advising them of their rights under the Constitution—is necessary to protect a suspect's rights. Although it happens rarely, some police officers use force and violence to obtain confessions. Requiring that suspects be advised of their rights before a confession is given ensures that the confession is voluntary, he maintains. In addition, claims that the *Miranda* warnings have freed thousands of criminals are unfounded. Levendosky concludes that the *Miranda* warning is necessary both to protect the suspect and law-enforcement officials. Levendosky is the editorial page editor for the *Casper Star-Tribune* (Wyoming).

As you read, consider the following questions:

1. What are the three elements of the *Miranda* warning, as cited by Levendosky?
2. According to Leonard W. Levy and as cited by the author, why is the right against self-incrimination inserted into the Fifth Amendment instead of the Sixth Amendment?
3. According to New York City police chief William Bratton, what effect has the *Miranda* ruling had on police and crime?

Charles Levendosky, "*Miranda* Promotes Confidence in Police," *North County Times*, January 9, 2000, p. F1.

Editor's Note: In June 2000, the U.S. Supreme Court upheld the Miranda *warning in* Dickerson v. United States.

In its decision in *Miranda vs. Arizona* (1966), the U.S. Supreme Court actually adopted the *Miranda* warning from criminal procedures already used by the FBI. The high court adopted the warning in order to safeguard the Fifth Amendment right against self-incrimination for those in police custody.

Three Essential Elements

The warning has three essential elements: A person taken into custody must be advised immediately that he has a right to remain silent, that anything he says may be used against him in a court of law and that he has the right to speak to a retained or court-appointed attorney before submitting to interrogation.

The court in the *Miranda* decision wrote: "Over the years the Federal Bureau of Investigation has compiled an exemplary record of effective law enforcement while advising any suspect or arrested person, at the outset of an interview. . . . A letter received from the Solicitor General in response to a question from the Bench makes it clear that the present pattern of warnings and respect for the rights of the individual followed as a practice by the FBI is consistent with the procedure which we delineate today."

In the First Congress, Sen. William Maclay of Pennsylvania spoke in opposition to a proposed law that would have compelled a person to be a witness against himself in civil cases: "Extorting evidence from any person was a species of torture. . . . The conscience was to be put on the rack; that forcing oaths or evidence from men, I consider equally tyrannical as extorting evidence by torture."

In his book, *Origins of the Bill of Rights*, pre-eminent constitutional scholar Leonard W. Levy maintains that the right against self-incrimination is inserted in the Fifth Amendment and not the Sixth Amendment because the framers of our Constitution did not want the right to be merely applied to a defendant during a trial.

The Sixth Amendment spells out the constitutional rights

of defendants in a criminal trial. Most of the clauses of the Fifth Amendment may be seen as protecting the rights of suspects or those accused prior to trial. In other words, the right against self-incrimination can be evoked when a person is still a suspect and not yet a defendant.

Physical Threats and Violence

The U.S. Supreme Court examined the question of whether confessions were coerced or voluntary long before it threw out the conviction of a black man who had been repeatedly hanged by his belt until unconscious then revived and questioned again until he confessed (*Brown vs. Mississippi*, 1936).

Though rare, in a few police precincts around the nation, physical threats and actual violence are still used to obtain confessions. When those methods are brought to the court's attention, those convictions are usually overturned. In a line of cases from the 1940s to the 1960s, the high court began to recognize that suspects needed to have an attorney present when they were taken into custody in order to preserve the fairness of a trial.

Pretrial interrogation is the stage when legal aid and advice are most critical to a suspect, said the court in its *Escobedo vs. Illinois* (1964) decision.

In the *Miranda* case, the court also recognized that the interrogation techniques as outlined in police manuals can lead to menacing psychological stratagems that undermine the right against self-incrimination.

Prior to the *Miranda* ruling, there were thousands of appeals regarding whether a confession was voluntary or not. Few reached the U.S. Supreme Court. Those appeals that did reach the court were mostly death penalty cases. After the high court mandated the *Miranda* warning, fewer appeals have been made based upon involuntary confessions.

A Watershed

In general, the *Miranda* warning acts as a watershed in determining the admission of a confession in a court of law. Was the suspect read his *Miranda* rights before he was interrogated? If not, in most circumstances, any confession would be suppressed.

When it rules in *Dickerson vs. United States* in 2000, if the Supreme Court decides to overturn its *Miranda* decision in favor of the less stringent standards regarding the voluntariness of confessions, which were passed by Congress in 1968, then a great many more appeals regarding confessions will reach the courts. And, once again, the high court will hear very few of them.

Sargent. © 1999 by *Austin American Statesman*. Reprinted by permission of Universal Press Syndicate.

Some claim that the *Miranda* decision has hampered police, that thousands of criminals have been let free and thousands of crimes go unsolved each year because of the requirement to read suspects their *Miranda* rights. Legal experts claim those assertions are phony.

Former New York City Police Commissioner William Bratton, in an interview with Michael Kramer of the New York *Daily News*, said that *Miranda* has not impeded police work: "The falling crime rates tell you that, if nothing else does."

Bratton made the argument that *Miranda* protects law enforcement officials from the suspicion that they coerced a confession from someone in their custody. Under *Miranda*, police have a suspect sign a paper saying he has been read his rights. Any defendant who then claims his confession was coerced has a harder time proving that in court.

Miranda strikes a balance in protecting a citizen's right against self-incrimination and protecting law enforcement officials from an unfair suspicion that back-room, third-degree techniques were used to obtain a confession.

We live in a constitutional, democratic republic where even the police must adhere to constitutional standards. And while the police solve crimes, they must still protect the civil rights of suspects. Without the public's trust, law enforcement is hampered. *Miranda* has helped establish that trust.

Miranda has worked for more than 30 years. It would be worse than foolish to dump it now.

5

VIEWPOINT

"The only people punished when evidence is excluded from trial are the victims of the criminal who will be set free."

The Exclusionary Rule Impedes Justice

Max Boot

Max Boot contends in the following viewpoint that discovering the truth should be the goal of the criminal justice system. However, defense attorneys try to keep the truth about their client's guilt from emerging during a trial. One way they do this is by invoking the exclusionary rule, which prohibits illegally seized evidence from being admitted at trial. Boot asserts that the exclusionary rule has allowed tens of thousands of criminals to go free every year. He maintains that the exclusionary rule does not protect innocent people—only the guilty. Boot is the editorial features writer of the *Wall Street Journal*, and author of *Out of Order: Arrogance, Corruption, and Incompetence on the Bench.*

As you read, consider the following questions:

1. What is the role of a defense lawyer, according to Alan Dershowitz, as cited by Boot?
2. What was the result of the Supreme Court ruling in *Mapp v. Ohio*, according to the author?
3. According to Paul Cassell, as cited by Boot, what percentage of criminal cases are lost due to the *Miranda* warning?

Max Boot, "Lies in Our Courtrooms," *American Enterprise*, May/June 1999.

An Irishman stopped before a grave in a cemetery whose tombstone declared:

"Here lies a lawyer and an honest man."

"An' who'd ever think," he murmured, "there'd be room for two men in that one little grave!"

The law [has an] uneasy relationship with the truth: Lawyers play hard to win, and they're supposed to, but there are lines they aren't supposed to cross, ethical obligations they oughtn't violate. Movies and TV celebrate the gamesmanship of the profession—the clever gambit that can win a million dollars or free a man charged with murder—but all that jousting and maneuvering is supposed to result in a noble goal: finding out what actually happened. It may seem paradoxical to assume that truth will result from the adversarial process, sort of like assuming a food fight will produce a delicious meal. But that's the premise of our legal system.

The Truth Gets Lost

How well is the system doing its job?. . . The answer is: not very well at all.

In the O.J. Simpson case, Johnnie Cochran managed to turn a mere murder trial into a referendum on racism in America. He skillfully shifted the focus from the overwhelming evidence of his client's guilt to Detective Mark Fuhrman's use of racial epithets. Indeed in closing arguments he even compared Fuhrman to Hitler. The overwhelmingly black jury was so determined to "send a message"—they only deliberated for four hours—that the question of who actually killed Nicole Brown Simpson and Ron Goldman (Colombian drug dealers? Kato Kaelin? the LAPD?) was all but forgotten. It was small consolation that Simpson was later held liable by a civil jury. . . .

Alan Dershowitz, one of America's most famous lawyers and a member of O.J. Simpson's Dream Team, instructs us in his book on the Simpson case that "'truth' is a far more complex goal than may appear at first blush." And: "Truth, although one important goal of the criminal trial, is not its only goal." Dershowitz is actually a critic of radical activists on law school campuses. But like many other lawyers, he glorifies the gladiatorial aspect of trials over the results. He thinks the "right" outcome is whatever the courts produce. He views his role as testing the prosecution's case, raising "reasonable doubts," and letting the chips (read: the truth) fall where they may: "When defense lawyers represent guilty clients—as most do, most of the time—their responsibility is to try, by all fair and ethical means, to prevent the truth about their client's guilt from emerging."

"Fair and Ethical"

The key here is "fair and ethical"—a concept whose meaning has shifted over time. In 1966 a law professor named Monroe Freedman wrote a pathbreaking article in the *Michigan Law Review* in which he argued that a lawyer was being perfectly ethical if he (1) tried to discredit "the reliability or credibility of an adverse witness whom you know to be telling the truth"; (2) put a witness on the stand "when you know he will commit perjury"; and (3) "give your client legal advice when you have reason to believe that the knowledge you give him will tempt him to commit perjury." This so outraged some judges, including future Chief Justice Warren Burger, that they tried to have Freedman disbarred. Yet nine years later when Freedman made the same arguments in book form the American Bar Association (ABA) gave him an award.

This reflected a larger shift within the profession. In 1986, for instance, the American Bar Association dropped from its ethical standards a provision that lawyers "should not misuse the power of cross examination or impeachment by employing it to discredit or undermine a witness if he knows the witness is testifying truthfully." It's still unethical under the ABA guidelines for a lawyer to countenance perjury by his client but this is usually circumvented by the lawyer simply not asking his client if he's guilty. It's clear that the legal profession has shifted away from truth-finding, toward "my client über alles." Thus many lawyers now see Johnnie Cochran's shameful demagoguery as a model of trial advocacy.

That's not to say defense lawyers should refuse to represent the guilty, or that the accused should not enjoy any protections. Our legal system does sometimes put other goods—

Freeing Guilty Criminals

The exclusionary rule has benefits only in the eyes of those who judge laws strictly by their intentions rather than their actual effects. The rule offers no civil-liberties benefits, only social cost. It artificially impedes justice by freeing at least 20,000 criminals each year. Statistical studies show that exclusionary rules, all else equal, are associated with a 15 per cent increase in crime rates.

The exclusionary rule has done more to undermine the Fourth Amendment than to protect it. As District of Columbia Circuit Judge Malcolm Wilkey once wrote: "If one were diabolically to attempt to invent a device designed slowly to undermine the substantive reach of the Fourth Amendment, it would be hard to do better than the exclusionary rule."

The exclusionary rule makes it more difficult to convict the guilty, including police officers who commit crimes. The rule makes it easy for corrupt cops to protect favored criminals from prosecution by simply making an illegal seizure.

Morgan O. Reynolds, *National Review*, May 15, 1995.

such as fairness and liberty—above the search for the truth. The Fifth Amendment protection against compelled self-incrimination comes to mind (although part of the rationale is that coerced confessions are not reliably true). And the common law has long recognized certain privileges, like attorney-client and doctor-patient, that also interfere with truth-finding. It's a balancing act: trying to punish the guilty versus protecting the innocent.

Departures from Common Law Tradition

But just as the prevailing view of the legal profession has swung against truth-finding in recent decades, so too have the rules of criminal procedure. The most detrimental developments in this regard have been two Warren Court decisions: *Mapp v. Ohio* and *Miranda v. Arizona.* The former imposed upon all state courts the exclusionary rule: Evidence seized illegally cannot be admitted at trial. The latter decision mandated that all policemen must read suspects their rights before interrogation; failure to comply is punished by excluding the resulting confession at trial. These are both radical departures from the common law tradition.

What price have we paid for making probative evidence inadmissible? Defenders of the system like Dershowitz claim that the impact of the exclusionary rule and *Miranda* has been minimal. But Paul Cassell, a law professor at the University of Utah, has conducted careful studies which show that *Miranda*, for one, resulted in a marked decrease in the number of crimes solved by police. Cassell estimates that 4 percent of criminal cases are lost due to *Miranda* alone, resulting in 28,000 cases against violent suspects and 79,000 cases against suspects in property crimes being dismissed every year. Cassell estimates that a roughly similar number of suspects receive reduced jail time because of these rulings.

Civil libertarians think this is a price worth paying to prevent rogue cops from preying upon the innocent. But it's hard to see how *Miranda* or *Mapp* does much to protect an innocent person—say a black motorist unjustly pulled over or a homeowner whose privacy is illegally violated. By definition there's no evidence to be excluded against a genuinely innocent person, no confession to be thrown out. Only the criminal benefits from the exclusion of evidence, and the bigger his crime the greater the benefit. Is there a deterrent effect to these rules? Perhaps, but bad men with badges are a lot more likely to be deterred by the prospect of being thrown in jail. The only people punished when evidence is excluded from trial are the victims of the criminal who will be set free.

The exclusionary rule and other procedural complications frustrate the search for justice another way: They make it extremely difficult and expensive to hold a trial, the principal fact-finding forum of our legal system. If any defense lawyer can tie a trial into knots, the incentive is to avoid a trial altogether. The result is that well over 90 percent of criminal cases are plea bargained instead. Plea bargains are a bonus for guilty defendants—they receive less jail time than they deserve—and a nightmare for the genuinely innocent: They can be bludgeoned by overzealous prosecutors into pleading guilty rather than face a longer sentence after trial. If trials were streamlined so that they focused more on the truth and less on endless procedural haggles, the courts might do a better job of sorting out the guilty from the innocent.

6 VIEWPOINT

"Where courts do not employ the exclusionary rule, the problem of police lawlessness gets worse."

The Exclusionary Rule Should Not Be Abolished

Timothy Lynch

Evidence that is seized illegally by police is inadmissible in court under the exclusionary rule of the Fourth Amendment. In the following viewpoint, Timothy Lynch argues that congressional attempts to pass laws to prevent courts from dismissing illegal evidence are actually attacks on the judiciary's powers. The exclusionary rule allows the court to check the lawlessness of the police. If the police make an illegal search, the court punishes the misbehavior the only way it can—by excluding the evidence from the trial. Lynch contends that any attempt to restrict the exclusionary rule must be vigorously fought. Lynch is associate director of the Cato Institute's Center for Constitutional Studies.

As you read, consider the following questions:

1. On what grounds do conservatives oppose the exclusionary rule, according to the author?
2. When does the judicial branch become aware of the circumstances surrounding a warrantless search, according to Lynch?
3. What is the substitute offered by critics of the exclusionary rule, as cited by Lynch?

Timothy Lynch, "In Defense of the Exclusionary Rule," *USA Today*, July 1999.

The Fourth Amendment to the U.S. Constitution reads: "The right of the people to be secure in their persons, house, papers, and effects, against unreasonable searches and seizures, shall not be violated, and no Warrants shall issue, but upon probable cause, supported by Oath or affirmation, and particularly describing the place to be searched, and the persons or things to be seized." Like other amendments that constitute the Bill of Rights, it was written and ratified to protect the citizenry against overweening government, but none of those amendments is self-enforcing.

How the Rule Works

Much of the debate surrounding the enforcement of the Fourth Amendment has focused on the so-called exclusionary rule—on whether it is wise or constitutionally necessary. Under that rule, evidence obtained in violation of the Fourth Amendment is ordinarily inadmissable in a criminal trial. A quick example will illustrate how the rule operates. If a policeman got a tip that a particular person was a drug dealer, the officer might launch an investigation to determine if the allegation was true. However, if he decided to break into the suspect's home without a search warrant, his effort would be for naught. Even if the officer found drugs on the kitchen table, that evidence would be useless because the suspect's attorney could demand that the trial judge bar its admission as being illegally obtained. Without that evidence, prosecutors would be unable to prove a crime had occurred.

Conservatives often oppose the exclusionary rule as not grounded in the Constitution, not a deterrent to police misconduct, and not helpful in the search for truth in criminal proceedings. They believe there are more sensible ways to handle law enforcement abuses. Liberals, on the other hand, generally have defended the exclusionary rule, both as an appropriate judicial remedy for Fourth Amendment violations and because it can operate to deter police misconduct. A closer examination of the issue will show that the rule is fundamentally sound, although for somewhat different reasons than liberal legal scholars typically offer.

The exclusionary rule can be justified on the basis of separation-of-powers principles. When agents of the executive branch (the police) disregard the terms of search warrants or attempt to bypass the warrant-issuing process altogether, the judicial branch can respond by checking such misbehavior, when it is able to do so. As it happens, the most opportune time to check that kind of executive branch mischief is when executive branch lawyers (prosecutors) attempt to introduce illegally seized evidence in court. Because the exclusionary rule helps the judiciary to uphold the integrity of its warrant-issuing process, it is an inestimable weapon against executive branch transgressions.

One way in which the executive branch has sought to expand its search and seizure powers has been to deny the legal necessity of search warrants. Regardless of the reasons offered, it is a fact that police officers frequently choose to proceed with a search without applying for a warrant. Because judges and judicial magistrates are not on the scene when such searches take place, only much later does the judicial branch become aware of the circumstances surrounding a warrantless search—when prosecutors are in court seeking to present the evidence the police acquired during it. If the attorney for the accused contends that the search was unlawful and objects to the admission of illegally seized evidence, how should a trial judge respond? Should the evidence be excluded or admitted?

An Illegal Search

The Supreme Court addressed those questions in *Weeks v. United States* (1912). Weeks, who was suspected of illegal gambling activity, was taken into custody at his place of employment, while a separate group of police officers went to his home and entered it without his permission and without a search warrant. The police seized various books, papers, and letters and turned those items over to prosecutors. When prosecutors tried to introduce some of those incriminating papers at Weeks' trial, the defense attorney cited the peculiar circumstances of the search and lodged an objection. The trial court overruled the objection, allowing the prosecution to introduce the seized papers. Weeks was convicted, but he appealed his case all the way to the Supreme Court, arguing that the trial court's failure to exclude the incriminating papers was a legal error.

Because a warrant is not required for every search, the Court began its analysis by reviewing the limited instances whereby police may conduct searches without warrants. Finding none of those exceptions applicable to the case under review, the Court concluded that the search was unlawful and that the trial court should not have allowed prosecutors to introduce illegally seized evidence at trial:

> The United States Marshal could only have invaded the house of the accused when armed with a warrant issued as required by the Constitution, upon sworn information and describing with reasonable particularity the thing for which the search was to be made. Instead, he acted without sanction of law, doubtless prompted by the desire to bring further proof to the aid of the Government, and under color of his office undertook to make a seizure of private papers in direct violation of the constitutional prohibition against such action. . . . To sanction such [methods of evidence gathering] would be to affirm by judicial decision a manifest neglect if not an open defiance of the prohibitions of the Constitution, intended for the protection of the people against such unauthorized action.

The *Weeks* precedent makes sense. The Fourth Amendment manifests a preference for a procedure of antecedent justification that the police must follow before they can invade American homes or businesses. The exclusionary rule is a logical and necessary corollary to the principle of antecedent justification. Enforcement of the rule puts executive branch agents in the position they would have been in had there been no violation of the warrant clause. Thus, the exclusionary rule restores the equilibrium that the Fourth Amendment established.

A Fishing Expedition

The exclusionary rule also is appropriate where executive branch agents have obtained a search warrant, but then disregard its terms and conditions. Such misconduct is more common than many people think. In 1994, for example, a state judge in Oklahoma issued a warrant that authorized a search of the residence of Albert Foster. Consistent with the particularity requirement of the Fourth Amendment, the warrant specifically identified the items to be searched for and seized—four firearms (one Remington shotgun, one Taurus .38 special, and two .22-caliber Rugar carbines) and any marijuana they might find. Despite that, the officers executing the search seized the following items: several VCR machines; miscellaneous video equipment; a socket set; two bows and a sheath containing six arrows; a pair of green coveralls; a riding lawn mower; three garden tillers; a brown leather pouch containing miscellaneous gun shells; a holster; several stereo systems; a CB radio base station; two soft-tip microphones; several television sets with remote controls; a Dewalt heavy-duty drill; a Vivitar camera tripod; A Red Rider Daisy model BB-gun; a Corona machete in brown leather case; an Asahi Pentex Spotmatic Camera; A Bowie-type knife in a black sheath; a Yashica camera MAT-124; a black leather bag with tapes; a metal rod; a Westinghouse clock radio; five hunting knives; a box of pellets; a screwdriver set; three vehicles; and a small box containing old coins, knives, a watch, and jewelry.

A Small Price to Pay

Without the protection of the Fourth Amendment, society *is* the victim. The exclusionary rule exists to provide a powerful incentive for police officers to seek legal warrants, its *de facto* elimination only makes all citizens more vulnerable to illegitimate and abusive state power. Constitutional safeguards were not intended to protect criminals. On the contrary, limits on government power were meant to protect innocent people from unreasonable searches by requiring probable cause. If illegally obtained evidence is allowed, the words of the Fourth Amendment become hollow and meaningless. Conservatives who preach the value of limited government should realize this above all. The insignificant number of criminals who are set free on technicalities (most studies place this rate at under one percent) is a small price to pay for our liberties.

Jefferson Pooley, *Perspective*, April 1995.

When a court hearing was held to determine the legality of the search, one of the police officers admitted that it was standard practice for his department to conduct open-ended searches. Here is a telling excerpt from the transcript of the hearing:

Counsel: Would it be a fair statement that anything of value in that house was taken?

Martin: Yes, sir. . . .

Counsel: And would it be a fair statement that as long as you have been deputy in Sequoyah County that when you all do a search that this is the way in which it is conducted?

Martin: Yes, sir.

Counsel: You go in and look for everything that's there, for any leads or anything that might lead to something being stolen, or whatever?

Martin: Yes, sir.

Foster's defense attorney moved to suppress as evidence all of the property seized during the search. The trial court granted the defense motion because the police had "exhibited flagrant disregard for the terms of the warrant by conducting a wholesale seizure of Foster's property [which amounted] to a fishing expedition for the discovery of incriminating evidence."

Separation of Powers

The executive branch cannot be permitted to make a mockery of the search warrant. When law enforcement officers disregard the terms of a warrant, the Fourth Amendment's particularity requirement is undermined and a valid, specific warrant is transformed into a general warrant. The sole way the judiciary can maintain the integrity of its warrant-issuing process is by withholding its approval. The judicial branch cannot—and should not—rely on the executive branch to discipline its own agents.

The exclusionary rule fits neatly within the Constitution's separation-of-powers framework. The men who framed and ratified the Constitution recognized "the insufficiency of a mere parchment delineation of the boundaries" among the three branches of government. "The great security," wrote James Madison, "against a gradual concentration of the several powers in the same department consists in giving those who administer each department the necessary constitutional means and personal motives to resist encroachments of the others. The provision for defense must in this, as in all other cases, be made commensurate to the danger of attack."

The exclusionary rule is a "commensurate" judicial response to the executive branch's attack on the judiciary's warrant-issuing prerogative. As the California Supreme Court has noted, since "the very purpose of an illegal search and seizure is to get evidence to introduce at trial, the success of the lawless venture depends entirely on the court's lending its aid by allowing the evidence to be introduced." Withholding such "aid" in appropriate cases is a measured response to executive branch encroachment.

Important Policy Implications

The exclusionary rule always has been controversial. The most contentious question is whether it is grounded in the Constitution or is merely a "judicially created remedy" for Fourth Amendment violations. The resolution of that question has very important policy implications. If the exclusionary rule is grounded in the Constitution, the executive and legislative branches must live with it—no matter how much they may dislike it. If the exclusionary rule is not grounded in the Constitution, Congress could try to abrogate the rule.

The Supreme Court has wavered on the question of whether the exclusionary rule is embedded in the Constitution. Some of its interpretations have suggested that the rule is an inseparable corollary of the Fourth Amendment. Others have suggested that it is merely a judicially created rule of evidence that Congress might negate. The latter view seems to be the dominant position of the modern Court.

Attempts to Curtail the Exclusionary Rule

Conservative critics of the exclusionary rule have seized upon the notion that the rule is nothing more than a judicially created remedy. In the mid 1980s, the Department of Justice issued a report that urged Attorney General Edwin Meese and Pres. Ronald Reagan to pursue policies that would "result in the abolition of the exclusionary rule." In 1994, the Republicans' Contract with America featured various reforms for the criminal justice system—including a curtailment of the exclusionary rule.

When Republicans gained control of Congress in 1995, conservative legislators immediately set their sights on the exclusionary rule. Sen. Orrin Hatch (R.-Utah), chairman of the Senate Judiciary Committee, crafted the Republican crime bill, section 507(b) of which sought to completely eliminate the exclusionary rule in Federal criminal prosecutions. The new section of title 18 of the U.S. Code would have read:

> "Evidence obtained as a result of a search or seizure that is otherwise admissible in a Federal criminal proceeding shall not be excluded in a proceeding in a court of the United States on the ground that the search or seizure was in violation of the Fourth Amendment to the Constitution."

A Back-Door Assault

That legislative attempt to stop trial courts from excluding illegally seized evidence was a back-door assault on the judiciary's warrant-issuing prerogative. The legislature has been unable to vest the warrant-issuing power in the executive branch. It also has been unable to diminish that power by converting the warrant-issuing procedure into a rubber-stamping process for executive branch agents. Its latest effort, therefore, is to negate the power by stripping the judicial branch of the one tool—the exclusionary rule—that has been most effective in thwarting encroachment by executive branch agents. Yet, even that effort has failed thus far to win enough votes to succeed.

Despite those setbacks, many people in the legislative and executive branches are relentlessly pressing to limit the judicial role in searches and seizures by short-circuiting the warrant-issuing process. Abolishing the exclusionary rule would give executive branch agents a license to bypass the warrant application process and disregard the terms of search warrants. After collecting evidence in warrantless searches, police and prosecutors could enter court confident that the judge's hands would be tied by the new law, which says illegally seized evidence cannot be excluded in Federal proceedings.

A Substitute Remedy

Critics of the exclusionary rule often stress that they wish to replace it with "a more effective remedy" for illegal police searches. The substitute remedy typically offered is a civil damages action that would enable victims of unlawful searches to sue police departments for monetary damages. There are at least two responses to such a proposal.

First, it begs the central constitutional question. In order to accept the suggestion that the judiciary ought to surrender its exclusionary rule in exchange for enactment of a civil damages action, one must first accept the proposition that the rule has no constitutional dimension. For all of the reasons outlined above, that proposition is not acceptable. The exclusionary rule can be justified on the basis of separation-of-powers principles. The means Congress cannot negate the rule with legislation.

Second, history shows that, where courts do not employ the exclusionary rule, the problem of police lawlessness gets worse. When the exclusionary rule was not in effect in the state of Ohio, for example, the Cincinnati police force rarely applied for search warrants. In 1958, the police obtained three warrants; in 1959, none. Although civil trespass actions were available to victims of unlawful searches, the potential threat of a lawsuit had a negligible effect on police behavior. The pervasive attitude among police officers was that, if illegally seized evidence could be used in court, there was no reason to bother with the search warrant application process.

An Attack on Judicial Powers

Since many opponents of the exclusionary rule take the Constitution's text, structure, and history seriously, they would be well-advised to step back and rethink misguided initiatives—such as the Hatch bill—in light of separation-of-powers principles. Again, the general thrust behind the separation-of-powers doctrine "is that neither department may invade the province of the other and neither may control, direct, or restrain the action of the other." Legislative rules that seek to curtail or abolish the exclusionary rule represent an invasion of the judicial province.

On the surface, such proposals may appear to be simple rules of evidence. Beneath the surface, however, they are an attempt to transfer judicial power to the executive branch. That may not be the underlying motivation of some of the proponents, but that would unquestionably be the practical effect of a legislative abolition of the exclusionary rule. The legislature accomplishes that end by "directing" judicial officers and "restraining" them from exercising their constitutionally assigned responsibilities. Any legislative attempt to abrogate the exclusionary rule, therefore, should be declared null and void by the judiciary.

Periodical Bibliography

The following articles have been selected to supplement the diverse views presented in this chapter.

Laurence A. Benner — "Protecting Constitutional Rights in an Age of Anxiety," *Human Rights*, April 2002.

Alan Berlow — "Requiem for a Public Defender," *American Prospect*, June 5, 2000.

Jane Fritsch and David Rohde — "Lawyers Often Fail New York's Poor," *New York Times*, April 8, 2001.

Orrin G. Hatch — "*Miranda* Warnings and Voluntary Confessions Can Co-Exist," *Wall Street Journal*, December 13, 1999.

Bob Herbert — "Cheap Justice," *New York Times*, March 1, 1998.

Wendy Kaminer — "Victims Versus Suspects," *American Prospect*, March 13, 2000.

Alexander Nguyen — "The Assault on *Miranda*," *American Prospect*, March 27–April 10, 2000.

Greg Palast — "Ex-Con Game," *Harper's*, March 2001.

Roger Pilon — "Symposium: Should We Amend the Constitution to Protect Victims' Rights?" *Insight*, August 31, 1998.

Stephen J. Schulhofer — "Symposium: Should the High Court Let Police Avoid Giving the Miranda Warning?" *Insight*, May 15, 2000.

Megan Twohey — "Once a Felon, Never a Voter?" *National Journal*, January 6, 2001.

For Further Discussion

Chapter 1

1. According to the Commission to Reform the Federal Grand Jury, one reform being considered is permitting witnesses to bring their lawyers into the federal Grand Jury room during questioning. Since witnesses would not have to leave the Grand Jury room after every question to consult with their lawyers, this would speed the process and would not impede justice. James K. Robinson contends, however, that allowing attorneys into the Grand Jury room would threaten the proceeding's secrecy because lawyers working for large criminal organizations would inform their clients of what was said in the Grand Jury room. Which argument is presented most persuasively? Defend your answer using specific examples from the viewpoints.
2. Richard Hustad Miller and Vincent Bugliosi struggle over the ethics and morality of defending clients who are "obviously" guilty of a crime. Do you think it is ethical for Bugliosi to not represent clients he knows are guilty? Why or why not? What do you think the writers of the Bill of Rights meant when they wrote that the accused should have "the assistance of counsel" for his or her defense?
3. Military courts are not bound by many of the rules and regulations that govern civilian criminal justice courts; the federal government is able to interrogate, try, and execute the suspects with little regard for the guarantees established by the Constitution or Bill of Rights. Anne-Marie Slaughter maintains that this lack of safeguards could easily lead to wrongly convicting—and executing—innocent people. Do you agree with her contention that a foreign national suspected of terrorism against the United States has the same guarantee of civil rights as an American? Why or why not? What if the terrorist is an American citizen? Defend your answer.

Chapter 2

1. Both Morgan O. Reynolds and Marc Mauer agree that the crime rate has declined; however, they disagree over the reasons for the decline. Based on your reading of the viewpoints, do you think incarcerating criminals is responsible for the falling crime rate? Support your answer with examples from the viewpoints.
2. Eric Cohen's biggest complaint against drug courts—other than the fact that their effectiveness is unproven—is that they are

turning the American criminal justice system into "therapeutic jurisprudence." Do you agree with his assessment? Explain.

3. Charles Wampler maintains that prisons should focus on rehabilitation so that inmates can successfully reenter society. Does the fact that Wampler is a prison inmate lend more or less credibility to his argument? Why? Based on your reading of the viewpoints, do you think that Charles H. Logan would agree with Wampler's assessment that prison life is unduly harsh? Explain your answer.

Chapter 3

1. Robert Kelsey and Ted Westerman cite statistics that suggest that three-strikes laws are a cost-effective way to reduce crime, while Ryan S. King and Marc Mauer argue that the three-strikes laws may not be directly responsible. What evidence does each author give to support their viewpoints? Whose argument seems stronger? Defend your answer.
2. William Tucker cites statistics to support his claim that the death penalty deters crime. The American Civil Liberties Union contends that the death penalty is barbaric and discriminates against poor, Southern minorities. Which author's argument is most persuasive? Defend your answer.
3. Families Against Mandatory Minimums argues that nonviolent drug offenders receive unduly harsh sentences under mandatory minimum sentencing regulations. How does John Roth counter this claim? Do you agree or disagree with FAMM's view that mandatory minimum sentencing may result in excessive sentences? Explain your answer, giving specific examples from the viewpoints. Does the fact that Roth is chief of the Narcotic and Dangerous Drug section of the Department of Justice influence your assessment of his argument? Why or why not?

Chapter 4

1. George W. Bush argues that current laws are insufficient to protect the rights of crime victims and therefore a constitutional amendment is necessary. Roger Pilon contends that more than half the states have amended their state constitutions to include victims' rights, so adding an amendment to the U.S. Constitution is unnecessary. Based on their arguments, do you believe a victims' rights amendment is necessary? Support your answer.
2. Charles Levendosky argues that the *Miranda* warning protects law enforcement officials by ensuring that a confession is voluntary; thus, it is an important and necessary fixture in the Amer-

ican criminal justice system. Bruce Fein contends, on the other hand, that suspects can still give a voluntary confession without receiving the *Miranda* warning. Which argument do you find more persuasive? Explain.

3. Max Boot advocates a repeal of the exclusionary rule, charging that it thwarts justice by allowing guilty criminals to go free. Timothy Lynch argues that the exclusionary rule is necessary because it is the only way the judicial branch can keep the police from breaking the rules. Based on their arguments, do you think the exclusionary rule is necessary? Explain your answer using examples from the viewpoints.

Organizations to Contact

The editors have compiled the following list of organizations concerned with the issues debated in this book. The descriptions are derived from materials provided by the organizations. All have publications or information available for interested readers. The list was compiled on the date of publication of the present volume; the information provided here may change. Be aware that many organizations take several weeks or longer to respond to inquiries, so allow as much time as possible.

American Civil Liberties Union (ACLU)
125 Broad St., 18th Fl., New York, NY 10004
(212) 549-2500 • publications: (800) 775-ACLU (2258)
fax: (212) 549-2646
website: www.aclu.org

The ACLU is a national organization that works to defend Americans' civil rights as guaranteed by the U.S. Constitution. It provides legal defense, research, and education. Among the ACLU's numerous publications are the book *In Defense of American Liberties: A History of the ACLU*, the handbook *The Rights of Prisoners: A Comprehensive Guide to the Legal Rights of Prisoners Under Current Law*, and the briefing paper "Crime and Civil Liberties."

American Judicature Society
25 E. Washington St., Suite 1600, Chicago, IL 60602
(312) 558-6900
website: www.ajs.org

The society is made up of lawyers, judges, law teachers, and government officials who promote effective justice and combat court delays. The society conducts research, offers a consulting service, and publishes the magazine *Judicature*, and the editorials *Restoring Confidence in the Criminal Justice System* and *Preserving Liberty When the Nation Is at War.*

Campaign for an Effective Crime Policy
918 F St. NW, Suite 505, Washington, DC 20004
(202) 628-1903 • fax: (202) 628-1091
e-mail: staff@crimepolicy.org • website: www.crimepolicy.org

Coordinated by the Sentencing Project, the campaign favors alternative sentencing policies. Its purpose is to promote information, ideas, discussion, and debate about criminal justice policy. The campaign's core document is *A Call for a Rational Debate on Crime and Punishment.*

Cato Institute
1000 Massachusetts Ave. NW, Washington, DC 20001
(202) 842-0200 • fax: (202) 842-3490
e-mail: cato@cato.org • website: www.cato.org

The Cato Institute is a libertarian public policy research foundation. It evaluates government policies and offers reform proposals in its publication *Policy Analysis*. Topics include "Crime, Police, and Root Causes" and "Prison Blues: How America's Foolish Sentencing Policies Endanger Public Safety." In addition, the institute publishes the bimonthly newsletter *Cato Policy Report* and the triannual *Cato Journal*.

Citizens United for Rehabilitation of Errants (CURE)
PO Box 2310, National Capitol Station, Washington, DC 20013
(202) 789-2126
website: www.curenational.org

CURE is an organization that works to reduce crime through the reform of the criminal justice system. Its goals are to ensure that prisons are used only for individuals who absolutely require incarceration and that prisoners have all the resources necessary for rehabilitation. CURE publishes the monthly newsletter *Citizens Agenda* and various position papers.

Families Against Mandatory Minimums Foundation (FAMM)
1621 K St. NW, Suite 1400, Washington, DC 20006
(202) 822-6700 • fax: (202) 822-6704
e-mail: famm@famm.org • website: www.famm.org

FAMM is an educational organization that works to repeal mandatory minimum sentences. It provides legislators, the public, and the media with information on and analyses of minimum-sentencing laws. FAMM publishes the quarterly newsletter *FAMM-gram* and the fact sheets *Race and Mandatory Sentencing*, *Women and Mandatory Sentencing*, and *Crack and Powder Cocaine Sentencing*.

Heritage Foundation
214 Massachusetts Ave. NE, Washington, DC 20002
(202) 546-4400 • fax: (202) 546-8328
website: www.heritage.org

The Heritage Foundation is a conservative public policy research institute. It advocates tougher sentencing and the construction of more prisons as means to reduce crime. The foundation publishes the quarterly journal *Policy Review*, which occasionally contains articles addressing crime, and the research papers *The Facts About*

COPS: A Performance Overview of the Community Oriented Policing Services Program, *America's Prisons Are Full . . . of Criminals*, and *Young African-American Males: Continuing Victims of High Homicide Rates in Urban Communities.*

Justice Fellowship
PO Box 16069, Washington, DC 20041-6069
(703) 904-7312 • fax: (703) 478-9679
e-mail: mail@justicefellowship.org
website: www.justicefellowship.org

The Justice Fellowship is a national criminal justice reform organization that advocates victims' rights, alternatives to prison, and community involvement in the criminal justice system. It aims to make the criminal justice system more consistent with biblical teachings on justice. It publishes the brochures *A Case for Alternatives to Prison*, *A Case for Prison Industries*, *A Case for Victims' Rights*, and *Beyond Crime and Punishment: Restorative Justice*, as well as the quarterly newsletter *Justice Report.*

National Center for Victims of Crime
2000 M St. NW, Suite 480, Washington, DC 20036
(202) 467-8700 • fax: (202) 467-8701
website: www.ncvc.org

The NCVC works with grass-roots organizations and criminal justice agencies as an advocate for crime victims' rights. It is dedicated to helping crime victims and their families rebuild their lives. Its publications include *The Victims Rights Sourcebook* and the brief *The Rights of Crime Victims: Does Legal Protection Make a Difference?*

National Center on Institutions and Alternatives (NCIA)
3125 Mt. Vernon Ave., Alexandria, VA 22305
(703) 684-0373 • fax: (703) 684-6037
e-mail: ncia@igc.apc.org • website: www.ncianet.org/ncia

NCIA works to reduce the number of people institutionalized in prisons and mental hospitals. It favors the least restrictive forms of detention for juvenile offenders and opposes sentencing juveniles as adults and executing juvenile murderers. NCIA publishes the study *Darkness Closes In—National Study of Jail Suicides* and *Masking the Divide: How Officially Reported Prison Statistics Distort the Racial and Ethnic Realities of Prison Growth.*

National Institute of Justice (NIJ)
U.S. Department of Justice
PO Box 6000, Rockville, MD 20849-6000
(800) 851-3420 • (301) 519-5212
e-mail: askncjrs@ncjrs.org • website: www.ncjrs.org

NIJ is a research and development agency that documents crime and its control. It publishes and distributes information through the National Criminal Justice Reference Service, an international clearinghouse that provides information and research about criminal justice. NIJ publications include the bimonthly *National Institute of Justice Journal.*

Office for Victims of Crime (OVC)
U.S. Department of Justice
810 7th St. NW, Washington, DC 20531
800-627-6872
e-mail: askOVC@ojp.usdoj.gov
website: www.ojp.usdoj.gov/ovc

OVC seeks to ensure that a crime victim's rights are recognized and protected. It is working to change attitudes, policies, and practices to support justice and the rights of crime victims. Its publications include the fact sheet *What You Can Do If You Are a Victim of Crime*, and the report *Impact Statements: A Victim's Right to Speak, a Nation's Responsibility to Listen.*

The Rand Corporation
1700 Main St., PO Box 2138, Santa Monica, CA 90407-2138
(310) 393-0411 • fax: (310) 393-4818
website: www.rand.org

The Rand Corporation is an independent nonprofit organization engaged in research on national security issues and the public welfare. It conducts its work with support from federal, state, and local governments and from foundations and other philanthropic sources. Its publications include the book *Prison vs. Probation: Implications for Crime and Offender Recidivism* and the report "Three Strikes and You're Out: Estimated Benefits and Costs of California's New Mandatory-Sentencing Law."

The Sentencing Project
514 10th St. NW, Suite 1000, Washington, DC 20004
(202) 628-0871 • fax: (202) 628-1091
website: www.sentencingproject.org
e-mail: staff@sentencingproject.org

The project provides public defenders and other public officials with information on establishing and improving alternative sentencing programs. It promotes increased public understanding of the sentencing process and alternative sentencing programs. The project publishes the reports *Americans Behind Bars: A Comparison of International Rates of Incarceration*, *Invisible Punishment: The Collateral Consequences of Mass Imprisonment*, and *Young Black Men and the Criminal Justice System: A Growing National Problem.*

Bibliography of Books

Sasha Abramsky	*Hard Time Blues: How Politics Built a Prison Nation.* New York: St. Martin's, 2002.
Jabari Asim, ed.	*Not Guilty: Twelve Black Men Speak Out on Law, Justice, and Life.* New York: Amistad, 2001.
Mark Baker	*D.A.: Prosecutors in Their Own Words.* New York: Simon and Shuster, 1999.
David Cole	*No Equal Justice: Race and Class in the American Criminal Justice System.* New York: New Press, 1999.
Sarah DeCapua	*Serving on a Jury: A True Book.* New York: Children's, 2002.
Alan Dershowitz	*Letters to a Young Lawyer.* New York: Basic Books, 2001.
Marcus Dirk Dubber	*Victims in the War on Crime: The Use and Abuse of Victims' Rights.* New York: New York University Press, 2002.
William L. Dwyer	*In the Hands of the People: The Trial Jury's Origins, Triumphs, Troubles, and Future in American Democracy.* New York: Thomas Dunne, 2002.
Joel Dyer	*The Perpetual Prisoner Machine: How America Profits from Crime.* Boulder, CO: Westview, 2000.
Jeffrey Ferro	*Prisons and Jails: A Deterrent to Crime?* Farmington Hills, MI: Gale Group, 2002.
Sara Flaherty and Austin Sarat, eds.	*Victims and Victim's Rights.* Broomall, PA: Chelsea House, 1998.
James Alan Fox and Jack Levin	*The Will to Kill: Making Sense of Senseless Murder.* Boston: Allyn and Bacon, 2001.
Thomas Geoghegan	*In America's Court: How a Civil Lawyer Who Likes to Settle Stumbled into a Criminal Trial.* New York: New Press, 2002.
Raphael Goldman	*Capital Punishment.* Washington, DC: CQ Press, 2002.
Joseph Hallinan	*Going Up the River: Travels in a Prison Nation.* New York: Random House, 2001.
Noelle Hanrahan, ed.	*All Things Censored/Mumia Abu-Jamal.* New York: Seven Stories, 2000.
Peter G. Herman	*The American Prison System.* New York: H.W. Wilson, 2001.

James S. Hirsch — *Hurricane: The Miraculous Journey of Rubin Carter.* Thorndike, ME: Thorndike Press, 2000.

Victor E. Kappeler, Mark Blumberg, and Gary W. Potter, eds. — *The Mythology of Crime and Criminal Justice.* Prospect Heights, IL: Waveland, 2000.

Leonard W. Levy — *The Palladium of Justice: Origins of Trial by Jury.* Chicago: Ivan R. Dee, 1999.

Marc Mauer — *Race to Incarcerate.* New York: New Press, 1999.

David L. Myers — *Excluding Violent Youths from Juvenile Court: The Effectiveness of Legislative Waiver.* New York: LFB Scholarly Publishing, 2001.

Christian Parenti — *Lockdown America: Police and Prisons in the Age of Crisis.* New York: Verso Books, 2000.

Nicole Hahn Rafter and Debra L. Stanley — *Prisons in America: A Reference Handbook.* Santa Barbara, CA: ABC-CLIO, 1999.

Jeffrey H. Reiman — *The Rich Get Richer and the Poor Get Prison: Ideology, Class, and Criminal Justice.* Boston: Allyn and Bacon, 2000.

Mei Ling Rein — *Capital Punishment: Cruel and Unusual?* Detroit, MI: Gale Group, 2002.

Paul Craig Roberts and Lawrence M. Stratton — *The Tyranny of Good Intentions: How Prosecutors and Bureaucrats Are Trampling the Constitution in the Name of Justice.* Roseville, CA: Forum, 2000.

Barry Scheck, Peter Neufeld, and Jim Dwyer — *Actual Innocence: Five Days to Execution and Other Dispatches from the Wrongly Convicted.* New York: Doubleday, 2000.

T. Richard Snyder — *The Protestant Ethic and the Spirit of Punishment.* Grand Rapids, MI: William B. Eerdmans, 2000.

Kate Stith and José A. Cabranes — *Fear of Judging: Sentencing Guidelines in the Federal Courts.* Chicago: University of Chicago Press, 1998.

Dennis Sullivan and Larry Tifft — *Restorative Justice: Healing the Foundations of Our Everyday Lives.* Monsey, NY: Criminal Justice Press, 2001.

Peggy M. Tobolowsky — *Crime Victim Rights and Remedies.* Durham, NC: Carolina Academic Press, 2001.

Michael H. Tonry — *Sentencing Matters.* New York: Oxford University Press, 1997.

Index